W9-BPQ-112

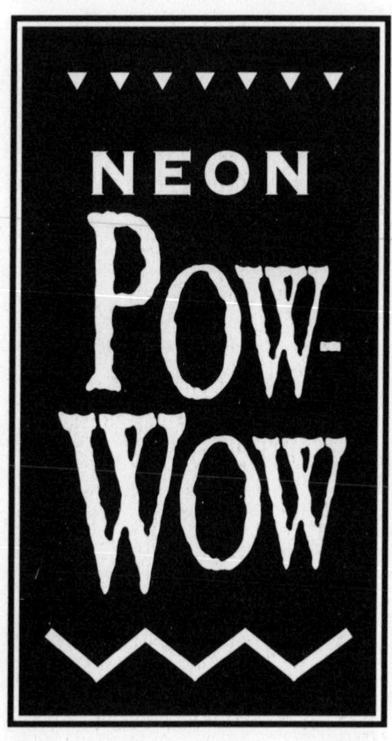
NEON
POW-
WOW

"Ałk'idą́ą́'jiní," she says. A long time ago it is said—ancient, magical words. She stops frequently to spit into the can she keeps by her bed. She does this with deliberation, so much a part of the telling. Long silences punctuate her stories, and we drift off into the world of her words.

From "The Blood Stone" by Irvin Morris

NEON POW-WOW

New Native American Voices of the Southwest

Edited by Anna Lee Walters

NORTHLAND PUBLISHING
A Justin Company

This book could not have been done without the assistance of the late Betti Arnold Albrecht. I also wish to thank Arthur Sze, Sue Bizade, and Vecenti de Gene Ortizio Juanajillo Alitizar.

FIRST EDITION
ISBN 0-87358-562-3
Library of Congress Catalog Card Number 93-8947

Cover design by David Jenney.
Text design by Rudy J. Ramos.

Library of Congress Cataloging-in-Publication Data Available

Manufactured and Printed in the United States of America

8-93/5M/0444

Contents

Introduction

A tradition shared by some southwestern tribal people, and told in their most ancient stories, is that the world in which we now live was not where the people started out. In a progression of worlds they came to this one. Also, centuries ago, the condition of the present world was prophesied in tribal teachings that warned of loss of tribal languages; domination of tribal people; turmoil within tribal groups and communities and without; a sweeping destructive behavior toward the natural world that would peculiarly mark this time period; and more. As a counterpart to these oppressive forecasts, the people were also given guidance on how they might uniquely survive the confusion and uncertainty of life now, honoring age-old tribal teachings and values that will always be applicable in any time period, despite the odds against the people's survival and some changes in their lifestyles.

One way the people have moved through these worlds and are able to survive as groups, families, clans, and bands, in the worst and best of times, is by formal and informal storytelling. Stories in themselves are tribal consciousness, as is storytelling. That the people and their stories are *one* has always been apparent to them, and their ways of life are also the ways of stories and storytellers. Therefore, the oldest stories of the first storytellers have continued to be passed on, reverently and irreverently, in the same way the first storytellers told them, because this is the way people and stories are now and have always been, reverent and irreverent, but also vibrant and expressive about their human condition over time.

This modern collection of work very much reflects this old and new tribal consciousness. The new work is still grounded in the older tribal worlds and traditions of the first storytellers. After all, this remains the foundation for the modern stories of contemporary tribal people. As an example, Irvin Morris describes in "The Blood Stone" one perspective of the modern world that is quite ancient and precedes his story by generations.

> There had been three worlds before this one, and this, the fourth world, the Glittering World, is the final one. Each of the previous worlds ended in cataclysm, its destruction brought about by the inhabitants.

The points of reference in oral tradition from which Morris, a *Diné* or Navajo, writes, and to which other Navajo writers in this collection also allude, are as real as if not more real than any event that has occurred in the last five hundred years, and they are the guideposts against which the modern world is set and experienced. They are not recently contrived inventions or devices incorporated into the works here simply for literary purposes or effects. When Della Frank says in her poem *"T'áá Diné Nishłi"*—"I am Navajo"—her pronouncement takes in all the older teachings and values of those previous experiences of the people on the way to the present.

An older identity and affiliation are clearly expressed here, separate and apart from an identification with predominant society even after five hundred years of living in it and interacting with it. Virtually all the Navajo writers' use of tribal language in this collection also brings to their work an integrity that English—*Bilagáana Bizaad*—might otherwise disguise or camouflage. In fact, in this collection the reader will begin to discover evidence of just how much some tribal groups are involved in teaching written tribal languages to their members right now. This is probably most notable, however, among the Navajos.

Of the twenty-three writers represented here, ten are Navajo or of Navajo descent. There are also two Apache writers and two Pueblo writers. The others represent tribes not historically associated with the Southwest, but they are nevertheless here, residing or working in New Mexico or Arizona. (For the purposes of this manuscript, Arizona and New Mexico comprise the Southwest.) The ages and backgrounds of the contributors vary. Half were born in the Southwest and others found their way here. Consequently, this collection represents a very modern mix of southwestern tribal residents, but this is appropriate and to be expected because of the mobility and urbanization in today's world. Also, for tribal people, it may be a result and an aftermath of fairly recent forced relocation, as well.

An interesting footnote to the preceding paragraph is my own reaction and response to the politics of doing a "southwestern" anthology. I am not originally from Arizona or New Mexico, and I am an Indian person with ancestors who were here long before boundaries were drawn across the continent and English names were bestowed upon places and territories that already had other names, before modern concepts of "Southwest Indians" and state boundary lines and residencies replaced older tribal concepts and visions of this continent as a living whole being not quartered and sectioned as the continent is today. Needless to say, as editor of this collection, I did pause and think about earlier worlds and the people's movement through them—particularly as I spoke to the writers included here and heard and read their stories over and over again. Then, caught in this flow of time and stories, it became clear again that what is most important is that the people continue their storytelling, formal and informal, oral and written, new and old, because these stories are animated things that have more power than modern politics. These stories have been around for millenia; modern-day society on this continent is very young.

Most contributors included in this anthology, "traditional southwestern" and not, are fairly new writers who have not yet been widely published. For about half, this is the first time they have been published. Several are in experimental stages, learning about a genre, learning a form, learning to speak, or learning a written language or languages. No matter at what stage they find themselves, they all express similar things about existence in the past and in the modern world. In terms of style, though, these writers go off in directions that heretofore have not been brought together quite like this. From Lorenzo Baca's "Ten Rounds" to Melissa A. Pope's "The Coffeemaker," there are many surprises in the variety of styles found here in poetry, short fiction, and playwriting. These selections of work were purposeful and carefully chosen to show a fuller range of contemporary Native American literature.

Finally, I want to end with a little story about how this book came to be. A few years ago, I had the pleasure of meeting a young woman at a university publishing conference in Reno, Nevada. Susan McDonald was then the editor-in-chief of Northland Press (now called Northland Publishing). Over the years, I became acquainted with other editorial staff there as I worked on various publishing projects. About four years ago, I met Betti Arnold, who later became Betti Albrecht, moved up the ladder at Northland, and assumed the job held earlier by Susan. In the meantime, Betti and I continued our acquaintance through correspondence and telephone calls. In the summer of 1992 I visited with her at "Returning the Gift," an important gathering of Indian writers at the University of Oklahoma. About six weeks after the conference, Betti called me to tell me how important she thought the conference had been and what she had observed and learned there. She also wanted to discuss an anthology of Native American writers of the Southwest that she had conceptualized. She said that she felt Native American literature has long been ignored in our part of the country and she wanted to change this. She was very excited about the project. Her enthusiasm was catching! She asked me to edit the anthology and prepare the manuscript.

Just less than a year passed from Betti's visualization of the book to the time it came off the press in the summer of 1993, a truly remarkable accomplishment given the talents required to make the book a reality. Sadly, Betti is not here to share the recognition for a project that she initiated. She passed away in March of 1993. Because I failed to thank her earlier for her commitment to this anthology, to bringing these particular writers to the forefront of Southwest Native American literature in this way, I'd like to do it now.

Thank you, Betti, for the honor of introducing these very fine new writers to the larger community. You really meant what you said and have shown it by taking your words a little further and making them a reality.

▼ ▼ ▼ ▼ ▼ ▼

T'AA DINÉ NISHŁI

Della Frank

I am that which is: A Navajo Person.
    This feeling is around, above, and below me . . .
I am the Beauty Way stories
    From long ago . . . when skies and land were clear
Before "misinterpretations" disrupted our ways, thoughts, and
    Lives as *T'áá Diné:* the Navajo People . . .
And I: Being of Female Origin, and He: Being of Male Origin . . .
Tenderly rise inside this round earth home: *Nihimá Bighan* . . .
    We put upon our feet: the moccasins.
And enclose in our hands, and with reverence
    We hold to you: the corn pollen . . .
We have risen at early dawn to greet Father Sun
    Warm, comforted and cuddled by rays of Gentle Spirits
Silently, slowly, constantly and gently turning
    We have welcomed the all-loving Mother Earth . . .
We sing songs: of despair, fear, and uncertainties . . .
And throw these sensation to the stars . . .
    In its place we welcome: inspiration, love and strength
To carry us through as *T'áá Diné:* the Navajo People . . .
We pray
    To Dawn of Summer Rain
    Reds of sunset
    And Whites of Corn Pollen
With garments made by Holy Beings
We ask Dark Swirling Clouds
To hear our humble voices
Ringing out in valleys, hills, and along canyon walls . . .
With renewed strength
We stand before you
In fine sash belts, silky shirts, and silver jewelry . . .
We pray
    To the east:

We ask that we reevaluate ourselves,
Our values, and our belief systems . . .
To the south:
We ask that we live long happy lives,
Perceiving aspects of "right" and "not right" decisions
and the consequences that await us with each decision . . .
To the west:
We ask that we remember our connections
To every other being by acknowledging our Clan Structure . . .
May we be humble to "Walks Around" and "Mexican Water" clans . . .
May we remember to set goals, according to our needs, wants, and wishes . . .
To the north:
We ask that we continue to have hope,
Respect, and perseverance: Of and about Nature . . .
We ask that we remain humble every day, toward one another . . .
May we always ask one another, "What are some ways . . .
To solve our daily problems as *T'áá Diné?*"
And may we through this process
Feel reassured of our capabilities . . .
With a profound respect for every other entity around us
With these thoughts in mind
Oh Great Spirit
We make our final turn
And again: Face the west
And thereupon re-enter our Hooghan . . .
And rest . . .

I am that which is: A Navajo Person . . .
T'áá Diné Nishłi.

▼ ▼ ▼ ▼ ▼ ▼

SQUATTERS

Irvin Morris

In a beam of sunlight streaming through a tear in the cardboard above, the woman's face appeared haggard, full of hollows and creases, though she was not yet old. Her eyes merely reflected the incoming light and added nothing of their own. This in contrast to the luminescence that would fill them for the man lying by her side, the man who was her companion and lover, whenever he smiled at her or said something that pleased her. Or touched her in the special way she liked.

But the man lying by her side only moaned and shuddered. At that, she momentarily ceased the slow back-and-forth sweep of her hand over his face to keep away the buzzing flies. She looked down for a moment and then looked away, resuming the mechanical fanning motion. He was not aware of her presence.

She had not been able to sleep for some time. Again and again she had seen the sun and the stars wheel across the sky. The feeling in her stomach kept her eyes open, though they saw nothing but the things only she could see in the air in front of her face. The sensation was that something was not as it should be in their makeshift home, behind the convenience store where they had camped ever since the street patrol told them to get off the streets or else.

So she sat there, in the depth of noon heat, sequestered in their hut of scavenged cardboard and odds and ends gathered from up and down the wash. Their sole luxury was a foam mattress found in a nearby field. It was on this bed that he lay, moaning now and then. He needed help desperately, she knew, but she could not will herself to leave his side. Instead, she remained rooted there, brushing away flies from his face, staring all the while into the air that swam with secret images.

The man in the store behind the counter knew they were there, and he watched them as surreptitiously as he watched his customers. He regarded them as squatters even though they were actually camped on a patch of no-man's-land on the other side of the wash marking the rear boundary of his property. He knew they had been there for some time, living in a cardboard hut and scavenging from his and others' dumpsters nearby. He never caught them at it, but he knew that much about them, anyway.

Often he would find himself caught up in a dilemma: whether or not to throw out a perfectly good loaf of week-old bread, a partial crate of overripe fruit, or whatever. Then he'd come to his senses and shake his head at whatever had possessed him to even consider the idea. It would be too much like he was condoning their wretched existence. It wasn't his fault they were there. They merely had gotten what they deserved, hanging around town without any money or legitimate business. If they really wanted to, they could go back to wherever it was they were from. Surely they had someplace; surely they had someone.

With that, the man would find it easier not to feel sorry for them. They were perfectly capable of walking to the highways leading out of town and out of his mind.

He had discovered their presence behind his store not long after the cardboard hut had appeared in the tangle of weeds and young Chinese elms crowding the sides of the wash. He investigated right away, poking his head into the shaded interior. He saw it was surprisingly clean for what it was. There was a weathered foam mattress, and a sack hung from the fork of a branch propping up the top of the hut. He knocked down the sack and spilled the contents onto the dirt floor. He was amused and repulsed by the things that fell out: a quarter-carcass of a barbecued chicken, a partially eaten microwave burrito, and some stale potato chips. He recognized the items as being the kind sold in his store, and for some reason that made him angry.

He kept a lookout for their return, and when he knew they were back, he stormed out there and told them to get the hell off his property or he would call the police. They responded to his threats with glum stares, which made his blood boil. "You should be ashamed of yourselves," he said, "living like animals, rummaging through my garbage for food." But they only stared, so he began tearing apart their flimsy hut. In his single-minded fury he did not see them walk away.

A few days later, he saw them again, sitting in the shade of saplings a couple hundred feet up the wash. Every day thereafter they moved closer and closer until eventually they had returned to the spot where their hut had been. One morning it reappeared, but he didn't bother to yell at them. They'd only stare dumbly and infuriate him with their silence. For the sake of his blood pressure, the only sensible thing to do was to ignore them as much as possible. And though he would never have admitted it, his bare tolerance for them gradually became something more like a proprietary interest in their whereabouts. It became something of a ritual to glance in their direction as he took out the trash in the mornings.

So they had stayed, dark shadows under the trees in back of his store.

She was patient and kept up her vigil, fanning away persistent flies. None of them would have a chance to land for even the briefest moment. But as vigilant as she was, her motions were listless. Without his voice to lead her, she seemed lost. He was an ordinary man, but he was good to her and she knew only to respond in kind. At one time he had been an imposing figure, she could see, because of the way he carried himself. She was content to remain in the background and admire the way he had with people.

He was an ordinary man, but he called her by a special name that had made her blush the first time he used it. She remembered the star-strewn sky and the sound of crickets and the weight of him gently crushing her as his breath burned her throat. She'd lain quietly next to him afterwards, listening to his breathing and feeling the cool night air move over her body.

But then he groaned again. She tugged at his shoulder and slowly turned him over on his side as he succumbed to a fit of coughing. In the mottled light he looked suddenly younger, and she heard herself answer his moans with those of her own.

She hadn't suspected, even when her menses had stopped. The pain and blood had come one night without warning. In the morning she carried the bloody rags into the hills and buried the bundle under a large juniper tree. He didn't ask about her long silences afterwards and gently touched the back of his hand to her cheek. He couldn't have known she was sick until she collapsed. It was he who had run out into the streets for help, and it was he who had folded her into the back of the squad car when it came.

She woke to the frowning face of a nurse who scolded as she cleaned her, admonishing her for not coming in sooner. Afterward, a doctor explained that she could no longer have children, and that it was her fault the infection had spread.

She drifted in and out of a fog for days, calling the names of people he did not know. Finally one day she could focus on the underbellies of clouds through the window. A few days later she followed him back out into the glare of the sun and trailed after him as he walked down the hill from the hospital. Her eyes drank in the sight of the land around her and it filled her with an intense longing that ballooned inside her, until with a shock she realized that she was floating right over his head. She rose high over the town and the surrounding hills, over the dry flat plains beyond, and onward toward the distant blue mountains. She skimmed over the rocky foothills and higher up onto the lushly forested summit, where the winds moved among the pines and the air was thickly scented with the smell of growing things. Wildfires and butterflies, iridescent birds and insects—all vied for her eye and she abandoned herself to the sensations.

But then she heard his voice calling her. Its warm timbre drew her back, bit by bit, until with a loud wail she hurtled back into his arms and sobbed.

The man in the store felt strangely agitated, and he paced back and forth behind the counter. He blamed the coffee for his restlessness and drummed his fingers on the countertop, grimly staring at the closed circuit television that showed the well-stocked shelves of his store from several different angles. Wordlessly he tended to the wild-looking men who came into the store with hands full of change for bottles of cologne and mouthwash.

She dabbed the spittle from his lips with the hem of her skirt, and in the same motion wiped his glistening forehead. He ground his teeth and shivered. After a while, she put his head into her lap and began crooning a melody she remembered from somewhere. Traffic droned in the background and the leaves of nearby trees rustled in a chance breeze. A group of schoolchildren passed in front of the store, laughing and chattering in high-pitched voices that faded slowly into the distance. He sighed deeply and stopped shivering. She looked down. The grasshoppers stopped clattering in the grass. His face had become a mask of youth so handsome her heart ached.

Just at that moment a sonic boom startled a flock of birds from nearby trees. They circled once overhead in a wide arc before flying away to the north. She felt the coarse texture of his hair between her fingers and sat looking down for a long time. At last, she got up and walked to the front of the store where the storekeeper noticed her standing.

He came out immediately and told her to move on, but the way she looked at him stopped him in his tracks. "Go on now," he said, "you and your friend both." But she merely stared like she didn't see him at all. "Go on," he repeated. "I'll go roust your friend. And this time I don't want you all coming back, you hear?" He walked around to the back of the store and slowly approached the squalid hut.

He heard the buzzing of the flies before he actually saw them. What he saw in the hut made him step back quickly and stumble back across the wash. "Jesus," he said, and swore under his breath. In his mind he saw clearly the emaciated body crawling with flies. He ran around the corner, meaning to grab the woman and call the police, but when he looked up and down the street, it was motionless as at dawn.

▼ ▼ ▼ ▼ ▼ ▼

YÉI TSOH (Crane)

Gertrude Walters

A Giant
Sits
Between
Black Hat
And
Window Rock
Tugging
At
Mother Earth.
Yéí tsoh
Tugs at her
Day and night.

When
I
Travel
Through
I hear
Mother Earth
Crying.

What
Is
She
To
Do
When
Her children
Have
Welcomed
This
Yéí tsoh?

▼ ▼ ▼ ▼ ▼ ▼

HITCHING

Carlson Vicenti

I wake up another morning dead. I have died many times, waking to this hell called America.

Rush hour. Denver, CO stains the light of the rising sun. A gray umber blanket of smog shrouds cold concrete and steel high rises. I sit up and shake the cockleburs from my hair. The Doppler shift of an iron stampede penetrates my ears. Wind from passing cars rustles the gray exhaust-singed grasses. A constant hum in my brain confuses me into thinking I am alive. I strain to breathe in an unhealthy dose of gases and toxins. Light reflects abalone-shell colors off of oil spilled into a creek of earth's milk. The water smells of gasoline and oil; fumes from the anuses of the steel horses fill my nostrils. I gather my backpack, climb to the road, and lean my home against the guardrail. There I sit, to extend my thumb for hours until it is numb.

The sun rises and the red and white blur of lights begins to end. The black veil that hides the truth of my surroundings is removed. Broken colored-glass bottles sparkle like diminished stars. Trash collects by the guardrail posts. A morbid black and gray factory spews out monstrous ghostly images that gather and disappear into the smog. White steam rhythmically puffs and hisses—the eager panting of industry and destruction. The air is thick and gaseous. Horses scream past on the highway paved over the bones of my ancestors. The town awakens to babies born, people dying. Distant pile drivers pound and echo in my thoughts. Workmen—spitting tobacco, telling crude racial jokes—pass gas and go about making a living for parricidal immigrant American families.

I am without luck—nobody dares pick up a hitchhiker in Denver—so I roll up a smoke. The sun's heat causes tar to seep out from cracks in the road. Tar is the leading cause of lung cancer in the world, and it is justice for millions of native people who have died because of imported diseases. I finish my prayers and offer the cigarette to the water. It floats and smolders. My creator pities me and I get a ride from a Chicano man going to Boulder. He has to go downtown first; I don't mind as long as I get out of this city.

In the depths of the pit, pale zombies slither the streets aimlessly. Ugly wretched mutants, inbred, lowlife, city-folk clutter, mirrored glass canyons built a mile high, and roads like Sheridan, Alameda, and Broadway extend like spider legs endlessly engulfing the earth. I am afraid lifeless eyes will fall out of dry withering skulls, chasing away and destroying the life I hide within me.

A dehumanized drunk Indian man stands on a street corner. His tattered, sweaty, dusty denim jacket hides a gangrene-colored bottle of T-bird from the police who serve and protect him from nothing. Stains of blood and vomit cover his pants. His hollow eyes glisten red. His skeleton protrudes beneath clinging deathly cirrhotic yellow skin. He is the product of the Machiavellian gifts of America: smallpox-infested blankets, the biological warfare of the past; Christianity's propaganda, savior of the dead, the infection and crucifixion of native spirituality; materialistic concepts—rich and poor, success and failure—that induce illnesses like greed, jealousy, envy. He is a wounded warrior, slipping from reality, escaping the nightmare to be another casualty of the final weapon of civilization. It is a weapon that kills women and children, takes away his desire to live and fight, to retain his true identity, and to believe what is right. Society uses the weapon to create stereotypes and misconceptions that cause disgust and hatred of Indian people, that help to deceive and manipulate Americans into justifying the injustice of broken treaties and genocide. Alcohol is the final ingredient added by this society to ensure Indians boil in a melting pot of poverty, oppression, and religious and racial prejudices. It is their secret weapon to hide their lies and insure the greedy manifestation of their destiny.

I see a fat, pink, sweaty white man, stuffed into a turquoise polyester double knit, an orange and brown paisley shirt, and white vinyl shoes, righteously spitting out evangelical quotes from the Bible, handing out pamphlets, and collecting change in a cigar box. His bright clothes and obnoxious preaching and the group of confused unearthly faces gathered around him nauseates me. They expect God's forgiveness after their ancestors tortured and killed their savior. It is easy to see by looking around at the state of man and planet—just watch Oprah, Geraldo, Sally Jesse Raphael—that Jesus doesn't hear their prayers.

The light changes and hundreds of singly occupied cars pack four lanes, creeping forward adding to our suffocation—Henry Ford's curse. We stop at a check cashing store on Colfax and the Chicano man runs in. He finishes his business and we head toward Boulder. He doesn't speak English well so we do not talk. Dark smoke billows on the horizon near the highway. Fire engines are stuck in traffic, their sirens screaming and yelping, and a fire burns in water. I cough up blood as an omen of my actions. I reach up and pull my eyelids closed and blood pours from my eyes. I can no longer see, just red. I hide my face from the man and watch the landscape pass.

Thousands of branchless, dry, oil-treated trees line the highways and roads, holding up voices on wire. Trees are not alive in this world. They make paper to fill minds with words. The spoken word no longer has meaning because the spirit of life is now meaningless. Traditions and legends are called myths and fables because believing in life has to be prayed for through books. The ancestors watching over the passage through life are called ghosts and feared. They are overlooked and ignored, never prayed to for strength and guidance. Paper wipes the crap of society and collects unseen in contagious landfills—dust under the carpet. It is pressed and hammered into prefab houses, the coffins of the living dead.

In the city the coffins are stacked one on top of another, twenty-four levels high, each one another story. Apartments are not apart, but are meant to house experiments in overpopulation and close confinement. Thousands of squirming rats, frustrated, eating each other, going crazy together, and the insanity gets worse, because masculinity means sexual prowess and a large family. Family is not the fruit growing on the tree that gives life, shelter, and shade when the heat of life's struggle torments one's thoughts. Instead of pity, adoption—caring for your second half so much that lifelong commitment is not a ball and chain, but an honor—men race to infect every inch of earth with the seeds of their image, watching unscrupulously as the planet is swallowed.

Rust-covered cars and machines are scattered and abandoned, collected in graveyards for salvation. The smell of horse manure is too putrid to bear, so Detroit must produce two million cars a year. Man's need for immediate travel is more important than enjoying each footstep, and the adventure has to come in doses that overwhelm the senses until you cannot appreciate the beauty of small wildflowers, the smell of clover, and the sound of the wind and the grass dancing.

It is better that obesity and lung cancer cause suffering, because breathing and walking a mile or more is far too strenuous to endure, and make no sense when life is governed by a machine that marks the passing of your life in a monotonous tick tock. The heartbeats of Mother Earth and your body are no longer sacred. They are just more facts of medical science and geology. Waiting for crops to grow and a pot to boil doesn't incite prayers for patience, but brings on images of Big Macs, the Colonel, and a pirate fisherman who steals your health and money—the money that drowns what there is to be grateful for in life—for possessions are far more important than lives. Getting from point A to point B in luxury; listening to CDs, cassettes, and LPs; watching images floating on waves, broadcast for your enjoyment, flying to the moon; having a weapon to ensure our destruction; all these are more important than the journey, singing aloud, watching clouds and stars, praying to the moon's spirit for help and comfort when you are alone, and feeding the world in peace. The planet is dying; crazy people are killing it. These people want the planet dead like themselves.

When we get to Boulder, he lets me off at Pearl Street Mall. It is early afternoon and people are returning from lunch. Yuppies and hippies share the same sidewalk, but never look each other in the face, because the yuppies don't want to see their 1960s reflections. They don't want to admit to selling out for Volvos, condos, and winter vacations in Cancún. They polish their shoes, cut their hair, and can't go anywhere without their American Express. They are so phony because they have the same lost culture as the hippies; just turn on the radio to KROC and they will both tap their feet and break into song. The closet Deadheads reveal themselves once they hear incorrect recording dates to songs; to them it's like making the wrong reference to a quote in the Bible. In one hundred years the Bible and the national anthem will have to be rewritten to include Jerry Garcia, Led Zeppelin, and the Stones.

I see a young couple; they have crazy his-and-hers haircuts. They look like Moe and Larry from the Three Stooges. She looks like Moe and he looks like Larry. They're both wearing nothing but black, hair dyed black, powdered white faces waxen and translucent like stale mayonnaise. It's around ninety-five degrees, and they're wearing black. They can't be seen in regular clothes because their friends might see them and crucify them. Their lives are as simple as that. Curious, I watch them walk down the street and up to a group of little Hitlers with razor-stubbled heads resembling decency and hiding white supremacy, racial discrimination, and violence. I can't understand what inferior mental condition brought on their state of superiority.

I get tired and hungry, so I sit on a bench and pull out some tuna and crackers. Everyone who passes looks at me as though I am a martian. My head feels like it is in a vice, causing my body to convulse in pain. I see a street bum walking around in rags asking for money. I pity him and give him an apple. He takes it, scrutinizes it, and walks on. I see him throw it in the garbage after he is far enough away from me.

A group of bald-headed men dressed in orange cloth and hitting tambourines and drums approaches me, and they give me a pamphlet and tell me my spirit is lost. I don't understand them because my spirituality is strong enough that I don't have to go door-to-door to recruit followers. I pity them that they have been brainwashed to believe they have claimed their spirit. I can't take anymore of this insanity, and I pick up my pack, deciding to go to Estes Park. The sun is slowly descending as I walk to the edge of town. I wait outside of Boulder, and a steady stream of cars flows past. It has been almost two hours and I am getting annoyed because people aren't picking me up. People are starting to assume all kinds of faces. Most of the trucks have old folk in them and they don't pick up hitchhikers. One old couple looks like two bleached prunes with sunglasses on, like the cover of *Tommy* by The Who except all shriveled up and white. Then I see Jed and Granny Clampet, and the wife and the farmer with the pitchfork in the painting *The American Gothic.* The sedans are usually rich Texans, and the Texans take on other faces. I swear the people in the last car were Walter Mondale and Geraldine Ferraro. Colorado is turning into the Texas highlands, and I am glad New Mexico has so many Indians and Chicanos because the Texans will stay away. I am totally disgusted with Texans; I get passed by them continuously. They come by in their new trucks and cars, yet they watch too much TV: *Cops, Dial 911, America's Most Wanted.* I become a psychokiller and I think of the lyrics to "Riders on the Storm": "If you give this man a ride, sweet memory will die, killer on the road." A car passes and a rat-faced boy waves at me to antagonize me, and I articulate a gesture of defiance with a flick of my middle digit. A rancher pulls up in a pickup and gives me a ride. His dog sits up front, and I sit in the back. The rancher is probably afraid I'll give the dog fleas. I sit back and think. In the course of two hours, I have seen every red-cheeked, bony, corn-fed, wholesome American caricature painted by Norman Rockwell.

I fall asleep on the drive to Estes Park. The sun is going down when we get there. The rancher drops me off by a carnival. I walk in and look at all the lights, games, and rides. Simple-minded crooked barkers yell out like auctioneers about prizes that can be won—pink long-necked Siamese cat dolls, Coors beer mirrors, and teddy bears made in Taiwan. Bells ring for a winner at the ring toss who lost five dollars to win a goldfish that will probably end up buried at sea—flush. Horns blare as the "Space Toboggan" hits top speed, spinning 'round and 'round; its rock and roll music has metal-head teenagers lining up to ride. Sirens roar at the "Scrambler" as children's faces are scattered, coming and going. Fearful screams fall from the mouths of people upside down in the "Hammer." The smells of cotton candy, corn dogs, hamburgers, and diesel drench the air. I buy a pink lemonade and drink it as I watch people wandering about finding thrills in life's complex machinery. I look down and find a twenty-five cent ticket. I pick it up but there isn't anything for a grown man to use it on. I finally see a sign, "Freak Show 25 Cents." I go in and I am shocked. A two-headed calf floats in yellow formaldehyde. A midget three feet tall reads Newsweek. He stands up and poses for me as I walk through. I pity his little soul for having to endure this evil world, watching it from a cage. The fat lady sits in a chair with layers of flesh draping over its edges. The bearded lady walks in her compartment, heaving her bosom forward. I wonder if she is really a man with tits, and if he is the secret lover to the fat lady. I see a little boy covered in fur from head to toe, and I can't stand to see another human treated so cruelly. I run out before I puke. Outside, it is dark except for chaotic flashing lights. Hideous eyes stare from pale demonic faces; heinous laughter and unnatural noises thunder in my head, crushing my sanity. My head pounds, my stomach sours, and I puke up the nightmare I live. I look up to breathe and a chubby redneck boy points his cotton candy cone at me and says, "Look Mom, an Indian man. Look Mom, an Indian man, look, Mom." She wrenches the boy's arm and drags him along, but I keep hearing him echo, "Look Mom, an Indian man. Look Mom, an Indian man. Look Mom, an Indian, an Indian, Indian, Indian."

▼ ▼ ▼ ▼ ▼ ▼

Alice's Rabbit Hole

GeorgeAnn Gregory

down alice's rabbit hole to the third world
far from the gentleness of red-rolling sand mesas
shaped by piñon-scented wind
to the world of perpetual auntie ems
and emerald green emptiness
even texas looks good from here
with its gentle wind-bent bluebonnets
and at least one good texas boy to fill a bed
there are no lazy-love
fly-buzzin' summer days here
to be
fanned by hot dry winds whispering
the coming fall

now I return with soft regrets
for a lakota man with pierced warrior chest
to be enveloped again in magic and mystery
at summer's end in misty red mountains

▼ ▼ ▼ ▼ ▼ ▼

San Lorenzo Day in Laguna

Lorenzo Baca

This story comes from my home in New Mexico. These Pueblos celebrate something Catholic, somewhat, but also Pueblo. We mix everything to make it work. I think it happens in all religions, anyway. Even if you swear by certain commandments, there are some you break. I think Pueblo people are really adaptable that way. My name is Lorenzo, so my saint's name is San Lorenzo. My son is Lorenzo, Leenkun Lorenzo Shpee Ye Wash Chee. The tradition goes pretty far back to when the Pueblo did a lot of farming, but the custom, the tradition, is still celebrated. It's my understanding that in the beginning, at a time of harvest, you had whatever you were growing—a lot of corn, squash, beans, peaches. You had some left over, and you'd go to neighbors and give them some. Somehow, that was tied into this celebration of the saint day on August 10—San Lorenzo Day.

On that day, everyone in the village of Laguna would have "Grab Day." You prepare for it. Everyone knows what day it will be, and families contribute things to give away: fruit, soda pop, all kinds of things.

When the day arrives, people meet at the house early. A man, like a town crier, announces through the whole village, "At the Atchees' they'll be throwin' at four o'clock, and at the Romeros', they'll be throwin' at five." It's very exciting—both when you throw, and when you grab. It's a fun event.

Well, for my son, his grandfather gives a speech and so we all go on top of the roof of the house because it's easier to throw, and the crier has already been out and announced. We take boxes of stuff, including water and water balloons, and put them all around the top of the roof. When it's close to the time, the family members start climbing the ladder to get to the roof—everyone, the grandmother, the fat ladies, everyone. Then the grandfather gives a speech and people start coming and they're all around. The grandfather starts his speech, thanking the people for being there and sharing in the prosperity. It's a celebration of ours for the prosperous year, good health, and so on, because we've been so lucky to have all this that we want to share it.

The grandfather introduces me by my Laguna Pueblo name. He introduces my son by his Laguna name. Grandfather is the first to throw something. But before that, he has a container of water, because the celebration has always begun and ended with water, which is very important to us in the Southwest. It's a blessing, a blessing of the people with water, very precious, but also a lot of fun, because people get wet. That's what the water balloons are for, and we have big jugs of water, so after the initial water blessing, it's just fun.

The grandfather throws the water out, and then my son throws some Crackerjacks, and then we all start throwing—just pitching in all directions—everything that we have. We throw dish rags, dish towels wrapped up, a beach ball, which is fun because people are jumping and trying to grab it, and it's bouncing all around.

And it's interesting that when people are catching or grabbing, you establish a little place around you, and you just stay there, and it comes to you, and people will call your name, and if you see someone in the crowd who's a Lorenzo or a Larry, then sometimes you'll select them out and say you have something special for them, or one of the grandmas. Or you'll have set aside a little basket special for them.

Well, one time I threw—I was just throwing, and my ring slipped off my finger and I saw it fly out into the crowd. I noticed it was gone, and I yelled out, "My ring!" And I don't know if this would happen any other place, but a man held it up and threw it back to me. I caught it and stuck it in my pocket.

In the excitement, you want everyone to share, so you make sure that everyone gets something. This goes on for ten minutes or so, and then it ends, and water is thrown, and you thank the people for coming.

Then we get down and see what we got. Then someone says, "Well, hurry up. Get your bags, the Romeros are going to throw." Then we go to the Romeros' house—the medicine man—and the same happens. You just dump things in your shirt, so you come walking out like a fat guy.

This is fun because Mr. Romero gives a speech and then has fry bread in plastic. When he threw it, the wind caught it and the plastic hooked up on the TV antenna, and everyone started cracking up. It was fun. Then they throw something else that is flat, and one of the women throws it, and it takes off like a Frisbee and lands behind the house. And then this tall guy, they say he's Laguna; maybe his mom is Cheyenne or something—see, we're not very tall—this real tall young guy, about six feet tall, came, and when the stuff starts flying toward us, he just reaches up and grabs it. The rest of us are jumping in the air, but he grabs the stuff. That's part of the fun. We laugh while he gets what he reaches for.

We go back to the house and have all kinds of stuff, taking a break to eat, and then heading out where someone else is throwing stuff. When we get there, people are still bringing stuff onto the roof. I notice there are some tourists standing back—two tall black men and two white girls—their girlfriends, I guess. And then things start to be thrown and we are all jumping and grabbing. I take a nice big jump and get myself a roll of paper towels, put it down, and get this and that. I notice the girls start moving up, crowding us, our space. They keep moving up, and of course the men move with them. And the girls get into it. It is exciting. But I see the difference. Pueblos are more reserved, I guess. But these girls just scream and the guys announce, "Man, did you see that?" You know, "Did you see what they threw over there? Wow, did you see that?" I mean, they're loud. People just look at them, tourists.

Then they start throwing cans of soda pop. And there are a lot of them, so I am catching and dodging, and then I see a can of soda go by, and I hear it, *pow!* I think it hit the ground, I'm busy catching my stuff. Then my friend says, "Give me those towels." So I watch the cans to catch them, and ask "What?" She says, "Over there." I look at one of the tall guys, who has a fancy haircut like they do in the cities, we knew he wasn't from around here, tourist. His head is shaved in lines and geometric designs. She rushes over to him, the one holding his head. He is full of blood, so she gives him some paper towels to hold on his head. We catch more stuff. This is going on over there.

Then they call Emily. She's a nurse. That is her job at the hospital. She examines his head and says he needs five stitches. I watch and grab. My friend gives him some more paper towels. He has them on his head. We can't help but laugh. They group together. The same people move back and start heading back to find their car. Everyone looks at each other, wonders about this poor guy holding bloody paper towels to his head. It is all quiet as we watch. Someone says, "It must have been his first time." Everybody laughs. It's his first time. Tourist. He is not Laguna, doesn't know about flying cans and such on San Lorenzo Day.

▼ ▼ ▼ ▼ ▼ ▼

Bringing Hannah Home

Esther G. Belin

we brought hannah home today
in afternoon sun with a crisp chill in the air
on a hill overlooking the bay.

two women with a child and a shovel and a frozen placenta wrapped in aluminum foil placed in a red plastic bag.
hannah was brought into this world
some say fourth others say fifth
five days before.
before we brought her home.

the weekend of rain softened the earth
but the cold discouraged the shovel from denting more than the surface.
i dug into the earth.
the ground weakened beneath the strength i put into the shovel
pounding the ground
smooth and moist at first
then cold and solid.

pounding the ground
warmed my arms.
i thought good thoughts for hannah and her mother
and prayed for us all
remembering those who have passed on and those to be born
and i thought of my children to be born
and i thought of my father who has passed on.

breaking into the cold ground
i thought of the day we brought my father home.
the winter of navajoland had frozen the ground
and the earth chipped like ice slivers of crunchy cold beneath our feet.
our bodies warmed by our work.

and the earth chipped like an old tree being chopped taking hours to finish.
our bodies tired from our work.
and the earth piled high beside the hole like the clouds and just as fluffy.
our bodies natural returning to the ground.

i dug into the ground
digging out earth that would nourish hannah
digging out life that would embody hannah
and soon a small hole appeared four feet deep.

there we stood
two women with a child and a shovel and a frozen placenta wrapped in aluminum foil placed in a red plastic bag.
the frozen mass of tissue and blood and life
was placed in the small hole
by hannah's mother.
and i felt her heat of tissue and blood and life
squatting with bloodied hands and cold earth
bringing hannah home.

▼ ▼ ▼ ▼ ▼ ▼

The Blood Stone

Irvin Morris

The plane rumbles down the runway, past weeds and grass and patches of bare earth. It climbs in a noisy arc around the granite cliffs and spires of the Sandias and begins the long journey over flatness. Snow-splotched mountains to the north and west dissolve in the haze, and the land turns from brown to green.

Hózhǫ́ naashá dooleeł, hózhǫ́ íishlaa dooleeł. 'Ayadíísh́į hózhǫ́ naashá, 'áyaadííshjį́ hózhǫ́ íishlaa.

I am rising on a sunbeam, traveling on a rainbow. I am going to meet my father, the Sun. I am holy with pollen. I am dressed in sacred jewels. Far to the west, *Tsoodził,* sacred mountain, passes, a mere anthill. *Yé'iitsoh* is dead. His blood congealed, solidified black. El Malpais.

"Complimentary snack, sir?" I shake my head. The smell of peanuts drifts through the cabin.

I am approaching the house of the Sun, steeling myself for the test to confirm my identity, when she returns.

"Would you care for a drink?" I look up and see my brown face reflected in her blue eyes.

"Some white wine, please." I reach into my pocket and scoop coins and bills onto the tray. A spot of red gleams amid the dull coins and crumpled bills.

"Is that jasper?" She smiles, setting down my glass.

"No, it's just an ordinary stone." As if it is an ordinary thing, carrying stones.

"Well, it's pretty."

The plane tips slightly to turn. Sunlight flashes on the wine and stone. The stone glows like a live coal.

"Díí nani'á dooleeł, shitsóí." I hear the words distinctly, as if they have been whispered in my ear.

"Lą'ígó hane' hólǫ́ ndi, ła'beedasína łá," she says. Hank Williams is singing about being so lonesome. Flames crackle in the barrel stove. A coffee can of sage and water perfumes the room with steam. The small stone nestles in the cup of her upturned palm like a drop of blood. It is egg-shaped, shiny, deep red with hints of copper. She closes her fist on it, curling her yellow-nailed thumb

over gnarled fingers. She is motionless for several moments, staring into her lap. Then she grasps my wrist. She shakes my hand flat and drops the stone onto my palm.

"Díí nani'á," she says, folding my fingers over it. I nod that I will.

"Nichei yę́ę sheiní'ą́ nt'ę́ę́." She smiles. The old man, her father, is twenty years dead. I hadn't thought about him in a long time. Now, he steps into my mind. Tall, ruddy, red-haired and blue-eyed in a land of brown-skinned, black-haired people.

"Ei hwééldigó na'isdee' yę́ę dą́ą' nízhdii'ą́ jiní." She points with her lips at my closed fist. The stone is warm from her touch. I remember the pictures I'd seen of the people huddled in brush shelters at Fort Sumner. They are ragged and thin. I am surprised to see that my thumb is rubbing the stone.

She is an archive. Countless nights we listened to her telling, captivated by the scenes she painted with her words. The ordinary landscape we knew—the desert, the mountains, the plains—transformed into a place where magic prevailed and monsters prowled.

There had been three worlds before this one, and this, the fourth world, the Glittering World, is the final one. Each of the previous worlds ended in cataclysm, its destruction brought about by the inhabitants. This time *łahgo nááhswdǫǫdááł.* A whole new existence we cannot imagine. No one knows except the Holy People, and they are keeping it a secret. Another emergence. *Hajíínéí,* when we emerged as *Diné* and the Hero Twins undertook the journey to meet their father, the Sun, carrying with them weapons of lightning and rainbows to do battle with *Yé'iitsoh,* the Giant. They rode into the sky on sunbeams and rainbows.

This is what the land must have been like from their vantage point in the sky, I think. *Sisnaajiní,* an anthill. And the land an archetypal tapestry, a work of brown and green and yellow and white.

Thin streamers of vapor swirl off the polished wings as we skim through clouds. Sunlight glints on the slick surfaces, on dents and rivets. Clouds pass like trees.

Hajíínéí. I do not question it. Her words are confident, rich with nasal tones, clicks, and glottal stops. *"Ałk'idą́ą' jiní,"* she says. A long time ago it is said—ancient, magical words. She stops frequently to spit into the can she keeps by her bed. She does this with deliberation, so much a part of the telling. Long silences punctuate her stories, and we drift off into the world of her words.

Then she shifts on her bed and the squeak of the springs is a summons.

"Nichei yę́ę́' ánínee'," she says. She reaches into her flour sack of belongings. She puts a pinch of Skoal in her cheek. The mole on her eyebrow bobs as her parchment lids blink. She puckers her lips and spits into the can. The clock on the table across the room ticks. A moth whirs around the kerosene lamp. Her calico cat leaps onto the tabletop and swats at the moth. *"Doo 'álhályą́ą́da, héi!"* she mutters with a shake of her head. Crazy thing.

I wait for her to continue the telling. The cat comes and purrs on her lap. Her hands caress it absently.

"Nichei yę́ę́' ájíníinee—"

A small boy is alone in the white sun. Sheep nibble on saltbush in the broad wash below. The only sounds are the tinkle of their bells and the occasional bleat of a lamb. A hawk circles overhead, dips, flaps higher, veers off to the north. The boy sings in a high-pitched voice. *"Nich'į'lá hǫ́ǫ́ghée' ndi, nich'įlá nízaad ndi . . . "* The words proclaim devotion of a sort he can't fully understand: The distance to your home may be far, and the journey arduous, but— The sheep dog comes to him, wagging its tail.

"Nísh 'ą́ąhnidishní."

Then the peace is shattered. Haashkiiłtsooí, his older brother, clatters down the rocky hillside behind him. His horse is dark with sweat. Its chest heaves. There is green foam on the bit.

"Tį'!" shouts his brother. *"Bilagáanaa bighiizh dę́ę́ yinééł!"* The boy gasps; fear squeezes his bowels. He pictures the soldiers spilling through the gap in the mountains.

His parents are waiting with four loaded packhorses. The cookfire is dead. A dark stain of grease on the ground buzzes with flies.

"Nóóda'í naalchį́'í ła' seesghį́, jiní." The broken body of the Ute scout had been found at the base of the cliffs lining the pass. The soldiers swarmed around it like angry ants. They are to be feared now more than ever. The packhorses toss their heads and snort. His mother says nothing. The boy looks at the peach trees his father planted and turns away.

Two months later, in the dead of winter, they are staggering east. They cross the Rio Grande at Albuquerque and file past the twin bell towers of the mission. The Pueblo neophytes come out to stare silently at the long column of dead-eyed people moving past. A girl tries to stop a soldier from selling her newborn to the Spanish villagers, and is killed. The boy screams at the sight of the girl's cleaved, bloody skull. His mother faints and has to be carried by his father. The soldier returns and hacks off the head. Let this be a lesson. A scrawny dog drags it away, to the amusement of the soldier. The boy cannot forget the sword for months afterward.

He learns to eat flour and beef on the arid plains in a bend of the Pecos. They build the fort under guard and channel the river to irrigate their crops. There are plagues of grasshoppers and worms and four years of drought. His father turns gaunt. His eyes grow vacant and he is unresponsive. In the spring of the fourth year, his mother's belly begins to grow, but there is no joy. At night, she thrashes and moans. He covers his ears not to hear, but he does anyway. *"Dooda! Dooda!"* she pleads with the hairy face looming over her, straining red, breathing liquor in her face. His father dies before the baby is born. After four days, his mother gathers rocks and piles them over the grave.

She keeps two things from that time: a red-haired, blue-eyed child, and a stone pried absentmindedly from the ground as they sat listening to the discussions about the treaty and the conditions of their release. The stone is red like blood, and she tucks it into the waistband of her skirt. Now and then she takes it out. Gradually, it acquires a polish from her hands.

We hit turbulence, and the plane shudders. We are between enormous thunderheads. Lightning leaps from cloud to cloud. The masses flicker like strobes. The man across the aisle laughs at the antics of Bill Murray on the small monitor overhead.

"Why don't you have it polished and mounted on a nice chain?" Skye says. She is watering the ferns this morning. She has neglected them and their edges are brown. They are not things I'd keep in my apartment. She is like that: forgetful, self-absorbed, but kind otherwise.

"We've been over this before," I say.

"It's just that I think it would be safer, that's all." That's another thing about Skye. She is transparent. I know it bothers her. I have seen the expression on her face, tight, a put-on smile. She'd rather I let go the tangible evidence of my background. Be American. She doesn't understand.

"It would be like wearing my mother's head around my neck," I say. Streams of water pour from the hanging planters and she scurries for bowls and pans. I pour coffee and wait. She is not finished.

"You know what I mean," she says. "It'll get scratched, carrying it around in your pocket." She is exaggerating. The stone rarely travels with me. Most of the time it keeps my underwear in the bureau. I know she contemplated theft—a friend snitched—but lost her nerve. How could she explain it when I have nothing worth stealing, least of all the stone? I know it scares her. It represents a part of my life that exists, and will continue to exist, without her. The stone must seem to her, after all, only a chunk of—quartz? It may contain the skin oils of my direct ancestors, but do I consider my skin oils a special blessing to pass on to my children?

"Jamie's friend asked about you." Skye wipes her hands on her T-shirt. "The anthropoid, I mean."

I smile. I can guess what's coming.

"He remembered you from the party. He told her about the way you had that little group in your palm. All you had to do was mention the stone." She bites her lip. It is an unconscious act. She looks wonderfully childlike. Her eyes search my face. What will I say? Will I compromise?

"Those anthropoids know the score," I say. They know how to namedrop. Chichen Itza. Machu Picchu. Chaco Canyon. I picture a pin dropping in slow motion and bouncing thunderously.

"That thing means more to you than—" She cannot finish the indictment. The coffee goes down like sand. I should explain to her in Navajo, I think.

"*Yáadilá,*" I say. "It's just a stone."

"I'm sorry." She sits beside me. *Dinétah* and Boston, I think, oil and water. A breeze turns the ferns slowly. I see that her nails are painted the same color as the stone.

The plane slices through the clouds. The stone is in my pocket, hidden, and the man across the aisle snores. I flip up the tray and signal the flight attendant. There is a brief moment in which I imagine that I am approaching myself. I am naked but for breechcloth and paint. I exude a wild, greasy smell. The attendant smiles. I give her my empty glass and watch her walk back down the aisle. Far below, Illinois natives see a glowing red stone hurtling through the sky.

The old man is nearly bald, but his blue eyes are clear. He looks at me and laughs. "*Héiyęę' ánít'į?*"

I identify myself. He thinks for a moment, snorting through progeny and relations. Then he nods. "*'Ą́ágí, 'áągí.*" He reaches out and grasps my clammy hand. I have come, boldly, to talk. Now I am at a loss. He waits, and I scratch one foot with the other. My knees poke through my jeans. He rests his hands on his cane. The pearl snaps on his western shirt gleam. His jeans are rolled up and a little toe sticks halfway out of one black sneaker.

" 'Ą́ą'?"

I am startled. What does an eight-year-old kid have to talk about? I swallow. A chicken squawks outside. Other kids shout. He closes his eyes and asks after my mother, my link to him. She is fine and so are my siblings, but what I wanted to ask was—I falter. He is listening! *"Ha'át'íílá béénílniih?"* A stupid question. What does he remember.

"Da'hwééldi dę́ę́'ná'íldee' yę́ędą́ą́'?" Yes, what was it like when they returned? *Hwééldi.* Fort Sumner.

I sit in the small, sage-scented room all afternoon. He makes tea and shares his cache of graham crackers. I am full as I leave his house. I try to picture him as a child. Did he wonder about his father? Did he feel the tug of some land across the ocean in his dreams? Did he rage at the Holy People?

I pick at the mushy disks on my plate—the promised medallions of beef, swimming in thin sauce. The sky flames yellow and orange and red as the sun drops below the horizon. The clouds glow like coral. Man-made constellations glimmer below. The man across the aisle licks his fingers.

"Yáah," I say.

"Excuse me, sir." Those blue eyes again, that non-stop smile. "We're about to land. Please fasten your seat belt."

I had fallen asleep. The city's spectacular skyline is framed in the window; the red lights atop the skyscrapers blink. I click my belt into place and my fingers brush the stone. *"Kǫ́ǫ́ náánéit'ash,"* I tell it. *"Náánéit'ah, yęę'."*

After the landing I walk down the corridor in a stream of chattering people. Eliseo shouts and hugs me. I laugh. We skirt regiments of yellow chairs and walk toward the escalator. He tells me about what has happened in my absence. Maria is sulking, he says, but he doesn't give a damn. She is getting too . . . too. He rolls his eyes. Ai, that woman!

"How was your trip?" He says finally, as we begin to slide down to the lower level.

"The folks are fine, bearing up well. I think they're relieved that she's gone, finally. You know what I mean."

Eliseo nods. "Si."

"I'm glad that I took this." I take out the stone. There is a commotion behind us. I turn just as two guys come hurtling down the escalator and crash past, knocking the stone out my hand. The stone bounces down the stairs and lands near the bottom. I watch as it drops between the moving teeth. Eliseo curses. An old woman above us moans. She has collapsed on the stairs. We are at her side in four steps. "My purse," she says. Someone stops the escalator and I hold her hand. There is a flurry of activity. I wait until the old woman is carried away on a stretcher. "Thank you," she says. "God bless you."

After they are gone, I fish in my pouch of pollen from my luggage and, ignoring stares and whispers, sprinkle a pinch on the spot where the stone vanished. Then we leave. Outside, it is warm and the air vibrates with the din of the city. We are quiet during the long drive to my apartment. The streets are lively on this Saturday night.

"Tell me a tale," says Eliseo. "Something that'll help me deal with an angry woman."

"A tall order," I say, swirling the brandy in my glass.

"A long time ago, there was a young man. He was in love with a girl who lived on a hill across the valley. But there was no hope, he knew, because the girl's father did not approve. They could just ignore him and get together, that was done in those days, but the father's blessing meant much to him. So he plotted elaborate strategies and began raising a bride price. His neighbors raised their eyebrows. Who in their right mind would want him? Who would want to subject themselves to ridicule and scorn? But love is unreasonable, if not indomitable.

"Finally the day comes that he has enough to offer for her hand. He dresses in his best velveteen shirt and brand-new Levis, silver concho belt, silver and turquoise bracelets, bowguard, rings, strands of coral and turquoise beads, turquoise nuggets dangling from his ears. He is magnificent. At least he thinks so, as he sets out on his best horse outfitted with his best saddle and trimmings. He practices what he will say as he ascends the hill to her home. A pack of mangy dogs charge at the top and bark and nip at the horse's hooves. They halt near the ramada. He feigns confidence, but a bead of sweat rolls down the side of his face. He wipes it quickly and clears his throat. Nothing happens. He blows his nose loudly, holding it between his fingers. Still nothing. He hacks and spits. Then he does it, tosses decorum out the window.

"'*Yá'át'ééh,'* he says, his voice higher than he'd intended. *'Yǫǫ́wehdi naních'įįdii!'* Get the hell away from here. He feels his heart curl like a sun-dried peach.

"He cannot go home, so he builds a fire over the lava rocks at the sweat lodge. He strips and sprawls in the sand. What is wrong with me, he wonders, looking at his naked limbs. He slams his fist into the sand. He is pale as a lizard's belly where the sun has not browned him, and his pubic hair blazes orange. He moans and tears at the hair on his chest and belly, and the pain brings him to his senses. He goes into the sweat lodge and sings. His songs are soaring hope.

"He does not go to her home again; instead, he throws himself into numbing physical labor. His mother's homestead, where he still lives, is transformed. Corrals springs out of the ground, two new *hooghan* appear. Her ramada, where she sits most days, is the envy of the local women. The livestock aren't neglected, either. The horses ripple and shine, the cattle bear fine calves, and his mother loses none of her sheep. The local men cannot help but notice. Maybe there is something to this guy, they think.

"The girl, too, has been watching. As the days pass, her resolve grows until finally, one day, she packs her belongings. Her father blusters and threatens—'You'll have freaks! He'll poison you with his blue eyes! You'll get sick, laying with that *Bilagáana!*'—but she doesn't listen. She walks down the hill one evening and appears to him out of the growing dusk as he sits outside smoking and contemplating the day. He leaps to his feet. They do not speak. They do not need to."

"Maybe Maria isn't so bad, after all," Eliseo says. "Maybe I'll give her another chance." He is jealous because she spoke to a stranger at the KC dance.

After Eliseo leaves, the apartment lapses into silence. I wander through the rooms. I am for a moment on the balcony. There is a breeze and it seems to fan the lights of the city. The sound of traffic is tedious. I do not answer the phone, though it rings and rings. I open the bureau drawer. For a moment my hand rests on the cloth inside, in the hollow where the stone once lay. Finally, I smooth over the depression and click on the lamp.

Tomorrow, Eliseo and Maria will drop by with some wine or something. Eliseo will pretend nothing happened, that he never said anything about Maria. And maybe, if they ask, I will tell a story.

▼ ▼ ▼ ▼ ▼ ▼

Noontime of My Life

GeorgeAnn Gregory

the ripeness of a sagittarian moon
calls me forth from my academic lair
its lustiness encircling my senses
already inflamed with the heat
of a watermelon july day
its beat pulsating my libido
the dying dutch elms
and the half-weeded backyard
its voice vibrating reality

on the eve of this new moon
what celestial mysteries
call me forth from self-imposed celibacy
the scent of lust catches me after fifteen years

sagittarian moon with leo rising
by those mythological hunters
you are too easily ensnared
producing at least one nuzzling cub
primitive fire
in a mid-melon summer sun
tsi'naajinii
his father's people
with fire and ice from his mom
the descendent of screaming blue-skinned warriors
melded with the mississippi mound peoples
of naniwaya
now walking barefoot through his mother corn
giver of life
brown as the earth upon which he walks
his eyes glistening green as his corngiver
mother of life

haa'shinilye'
my sagittarian moons
ghostly callings at the noontime of my life

The Turkey Tender

Karen and Wally Strong

Narrator: Long ago in the time of old Indian ways, an orphan girl lived among the people. She had no family to give her clothes or food, so she made her living by tending the community's flock of turkeys. Her name was Dathla.

Dathla: Time to get up! It's time to go out to the desert!
Turkey #1: All right! You heard her! Let's go!
Turkey #2: Everybody stay together!
Turkey #3: Line up! Line up!
Turkey #4: No! No! Just stay together!
Turkey #5: I want to sleep.
Turkey #6: I'm hungry!
Turkey #7: Oh! Shut up! Let's go!
Turkey #8: Wait for me!
(As the turkeys leave the corral, Dathla pets each one)

Narrator: The animal and people worlds were not that different in the time of old Indian ways. Dathla and the turkeys could talk to each other. She was very kind to all of the turkeys and knew each one by name.

(One turkey stumbles and falls, Dathla helps the turkey up)
Turkey #4: Ow!
Dathla: I'll help you!
Turkey #5: She is always here to help us!
Turkey #6: Yes! She is!

Narrator: Dathla has led the turkeys to food and water. Now she is going to sit down and spend the afternoon daydreaming.

Dathla: I talk to turkeys all day! I wonder what it is like to talk to people like me . . . and learn their dances and songs? *(falls asleep)*

Turkey #1:	I heard her!
Turkey #2:	So did I!
Turkey #3:	She wants to talk to people!
Turkey #7:	And she wants to learn their songs!
Turkey #8:	Yes! She wants to learn their dances, too!

Narrator: The turkeys are gathered together. They want to do Dathla a favor for all of the good things she has done for them.

Turkey #6:	Dathla has helped us! Let's help her!
Turkey #5:	How can we help her?
Turkey #4:	That's easy! We'll follow out her dreams!
Turkey #3:	Good! We'll send her to the ceremonial tomorrow!
Turkey #8:	Yeah! We can make her clothes look like new!
Turkey #2:	We can give her jewelry!
Turkey #7:	We can make her a feather headdress!
Turkey #1:	What are we waiting for!

Narrator: Dathla had always been along with the turkeys. Now the turkeys were going to give her a chance to mingle with the people!

(Dathla wakes up)

Dathla: Okay! Let's go home!

(Dathla closes the gate of the corral where the turkeys sleep)

Dathla:	Good morning, my turkey friends!
All Turkeys:	Good morning, Dathla!

Narrator: Dathla leads the turkeys to food and chuush. The turkeys circle Dathla.

All Turkeys:	Surprise! Surprise!
Turkey #8:	Dathla! We have a surprise for you!
Turkey #7:	We heard your dream!
Turkey #6:	We are sending you to the ceremonial today!
Dathla:	I can't go! I can't leave you! And I have no clothes!
Turkey #5:	We know the way home!
Turkey #4:	We have gifts for you!

Turkey #3: Hold still!

Narrator: The turkeys move closer and begin pecking and pecking and pecking. They aren't pecking her very hard, but she can feel them and they are tickling her and she is laughing.

Turkey #2: Your buckskin is pretty again!
Turkey #1: It feels so soft!
Turkey #8: Here are your beads!
Turkey #7: We found them at the pawnshop!
Turkey #6: No! No! We found the beads . . .
Turkey #5: . . . and put them together ourselves!
Turkey #4: Here is your feather headdress!
Dathla: Oh! Thank you!
(She turns to leave)

Narrator: Before Dathla leaves, the turkeys caution her to return before sundown to open the corral gate. The turkeys know the way home, but they can't open the gate themselves. Dathla can hear the people singing as she nears the ceremonial.

(Dancing and singing)
Girl #1: Who is she?
Girl #2: I don't know. I haven't seen her before.
Girl #3: Let's go and talk to her!

(The girls walk up and greet Dathla)
Girl #4: *Yá'át'ééh!*
Girl #1: Come and join us in our dances!

Narrator: Dathla joins the dancing.

(Another song)

Narrator: Dathla has forgotten the turkeys' wish for her to return to open the corral gate.

Dathla: I'm having so much fun! I wish this day could last forever!

Narrator: The day was almost over when the Chief's son came up to Dathla and asked her to dance.

Chief's Son: Will you dance with me?
Dathla: Yes!
Chief's Son: Where are you from?
Dathla: I can't tell you.
Chief's Son: Who is your family?
Dathla: I can't tell you that either!
Chief's Son: What is happening to your clothes?

Narrator: Dathla's buckskin begins matting from the hours of dancing. The fringes become all uneven, and the seams are falling apart again.

Dathla: Oh, no! I wish I had a few minutes more.
(Song)

Narrator: All the turkeys' beautiful hard work begins to fall apart. Dathla's feather headdress flies away and the beads scatter over the ground. Dathla flees the circle.

Dathla: Oh, no! It's late! I hope the turkeys are still waiting!
All turkeys: She betrayed our trust! Let us find another home in the forest!
(Turkeys leave in all directions)

Narrator: Dathla has lost the turkeys. They have become wild. All she can find are their tracks in the foothills leading into the forest. Now Dathla, the orphan girl, is truly all alone.

(Five minutes more, song, everyone)

▼ ▼ ▼ ▼ ▼ ▼

BLUES-ING ON THE BROWN VIBE

Esther G. Belin

I.
and coyote struts down east 14th
feeling good
looking good
feeling the brown
melting into the brown that loiters
rapping with the brown in front of the native american health center
talking that talk
of relocation from tribal nation
of recent immigration to the place some call the united states
home to many dislocated funky brown

ironic immigration

more accurate tribal nation to tribal nation

and coyote sprinkles corn pollen in the four directions
to thank the tribal police
    indigenous to what some call the state of california
    the city of oakland
for allowing use of their land

II.
and coyote travels by greyhound from albuquerque, NM, USA through
navajoland
to oakland, CA, USA
laughing
interstate 40 is cluttered with RVs from as far away as maine
traveling and traveling
to perpetuate the myth
coyote kicks back for most of the ride
amused by the constant herd of tourists

amazed by the mythic indian they create
at a pit stop in winslow
coyote trades a worn beaded cigarette lighter for roasted corn
from a middle-aged navajo woman squatting
in front of a store

and coyote squats alongside the woman
talking that talk
of bordertown blues
of reservation discrimination
blues-ing on the brown vibe
a *bilagáana* snaps a photo
the navajo woman stands
holding out her hand
requesting some of her soul back
instead
she gets a worn picture of george washington on a dollar bill

and coyote starts on another ear of corn
climbing onto the greyhound
the woman
still squatting
waiting
tired of learning not to want
waits there for the return of all her pieces

III.
and coyote wanders
right into a ponca sitting at the fruitvale bart station
next to the ponca is a seminole
coyote struts up to the two
"where ya'all from?"

the ponca replies
"oooklahooma"
pause
the seminole silent watches a rush of people
climb in and out of the train headed for fremont

the seminole stretches his arms up and back stiff from the wooden benches
pause
he pushes his lips out toward the ponca
slowly gesturing that he too is from oklahoma

coyote wonders
"where 'bouts?"

the ponca replies
"ponnca city"
pause
the seminole replies
"seminoole"

coyote gestures to the ponca
"you ponca?"
the ponca nods his head in affirmation
coyote nods his head in contentment
to the seminole
coyote asks
"you seminole?"
pause
the seminole now watching some kids eating frozen fruit bars
nods his head

and coyote shares his smokes with the two
and ten minutes later
they travel together on the richmond train
headed for wednesday night dinner at the intertribal friendship house

IV.
and coyote blues-ing on the urban brown funk vibe
wanders
in and out of existence
tasting the brown
rusty at times
worn bitter from relocation.

▼ ▼ ▼ ▼ ▼ ▼

A World Before the Bilagáana

Patroclus Eugene Savino

I

Tall Boy ran toward the vast mountain that rose high into the gloomy sky. His stride was long and supple as his warm brown eyes leaped ahead into the mist, searching for the dimly lit trail. The suffocating agony of his harsh breathing increased as he got closer to the mountain. His entire body felt light, like the feathers of the bald eagles that touch the soft clouds. The cool Mother Earth gave his legs more strength to continue up the trail to meet the gods of the morning.

His eyes widened and sparkled as he watched the dawn fling her baby blue scarf against the eastern horizon. The light began to flood the vast heaven, enveloping the tiny stars that covered the universe and replacing it with a huge array of colors. One beautiful star of dawn held on a little longer while others faded into a new day.

Down in the valley the silhouette of lonely trees rose from the black mist that covered the sleeping Mother Earth. They stood among the sagebrush, their trunks twisted by the wild winds of the distant prairielands of the west, their branches spreading to the heavens. A cool breeze swept up toward the mountains and shook the leaves with the sweet fragrance of a distant storm. The crystal clear dew on the leaves ran down the stems as the sleeping flowers were swayed by the soft breeze.

He stood high upon a flat rock as his eyes roamed into the changing heavens and upon the darkness that covered the sleeping Mother Earth. He heard only the pounding of his heart and the agony of his harsh breathing. He felt his stomach twist and turn to get rid of the vile taste that came from his belly, but he knew this was not the time or the place to let it out. He forced his mind to think of the things he had to do once he got home. The cool sweat ran down his broad shoulders and onto his firm, round buttocks.

His silhouette stood out against the changing sky as he raised his arms to the morning gods. Tall Boy gave some of the yellow pollen and received the blessing from the gods of the dawn. He uttered his morning prayer in his deep voice and it echoed far into the silent, sleeping world:

Changing Woman, My Mother
Dawn Boy, Dawn Girl
White Corn Boy, Yellow Corn Girl
White Shell Woman
Mother of Dawn
People of Dawn
Led me into the path of beauty,
Sprinkled with the yellow pollen
White corn upon my path
The path that I set my feet upon
Into the dawning of tomorrow.
Protect me . . . my soul . . .
From the evil spirits that emerged from
nowhere
As I travel upon the path of beauty
To have the strength
To withstand the black evil spirit . . .
May the beauty surround me
In front . . . behind . . . on the sides
Above me and beneath me
Into the beauty that is before me,
and after me
In beauty . . . In beauty
May I be filled with beauty
In beauty
Finished in Beauty.

The huge forms of dark monsters that seemed to rise out of the dark valley soon vanished as the bright shining hair of the sun unfolded upon Mother Earth. The darkness withdrew to the west along with the stars. Somewhere out in a distant valley a coyote let out the last cry of the day. The morning dove sang its pre-dawn music to the sleeping creatures, and it penetrated their dreams.

Tall Boy ran down to the icy cold waterfall and jumped beneath it before giving a second thought about how cold the water was. It poured upon his head, down his broad chest and into the lines and curves of his abdomen. His tensed body relaxed and felt a warm hand surround it. He felt all parts of his body as though he never knew they were there all this time. His legs and arms were hard as rocks and he thought of all the mornings he had been jerked out of his warm bed to be sent out into the icy cold winter morning or the early morning showers. He remembered the words of his grandfather, who seemed to repeat himself every morning: "Young man, get out of bed while the day is still young. Run to the east and welcome the new day. Be among the gods of dawn, give them your pollen, and in return they will bless you with a richer life and shield you from the evil spirits. They linger just about anywhere you go and emerge out of nowhere, to overcome you and make you come short of what you want out of your life. So beware of this, my grandson. Rise early with the dawn people and walk with them in the fresh cool air of the day. Overcome the evil, be strong, and stand on your own two feet." Tall Boy got out of the waterfall, wrung out his long black hair and shook it. He made sure the tiny bag that held the yellow pollen was still attached to the long strip of deer skin that went around his neck. He wiped the water buds from his body and chills invaded him. "I must continue on home before it gets any brighter and grandfather becomes angry with me for being so slow. But I feel a lot better now after the cold morning shower," he thought as he looked into the thick forest. "Why do I have a sudden feeling that someone is looking at my body?"

He shook his hair for the last time and retraced the trail down into the valley. The tree branches seemed to reach out to his body as he continued to run without glancing sideways. "I will be all right once I cross the wide washes in the valley," he thought as he glanced up at the sky. "From there it is not far to my home, and I can see grandpa standing outside with an angry expression on his dark face. Those trees and sagebrushes—I thought I had already passed them back there. Ah—I must be thinking too far ahead now. Now, I am near the wide wash. . . . I can see the tall yellow-green shrubs growing along the dry river bed."

Tall Boy felt a big knot form inside his stomach as he went down to the bottom of the wash bed. His eyes became wide as he inhaled the breeze that froze his entire body. His mind went blank and time appeared to stop at that moment.

There in his path sat a hideous-looking man who was half naked. The man had taken a brown bear skin from his shoulders and wrapped it around his waist.

"*Yá'át'ééh,*" said the man-wolf with a grin drawn across his painted face. His evil eyes sparkled and captured Tall Boy's attention as they studied his nude body. The man-wolf waited for the young fellow to utter a single word and when he did not, he continued. "Fate has brought us together again, young man. You have matured since the last time I saw you with your grandfather. Your strong body and soul have awakened my weary mind and I have longed for you. Now I have you in the palm of my hands, just where I wanted you to be." He touched the turquoise and shell necklaces that crisscrossed his chest. He continued to gaze into the youth's eyes. "I see you are struggling against my power, but it won't be long before you yield. Your strength is slowly fading. Nothing . . . nothing can break my strong spell over you now. I have the power to kill you quickly or torture your body and mind, to make you feel the agony of dying."

Tiny beads of sweat ran down the young man's face, and his chest expanded, inhaling the strong odor that surrounded the wolf-man. Tall Boy felt he was becoming smaller and smaller. He struggled each moment in his mind, trying to grab the thin line that ran between life and death. The voice of the evil man penetrated his blank mind and each word lingered a little bit longer than the previous word. His eyes felt as though they were frozen, staring at the colorful man's face.

"I have heard so much praise about you that it cuts deep into my flesh, and it takes a long time before it heals. I did not get the others and I don't intend to return home without accomplishing anything . . . " said the wicked man as he ran his fingers through his long silver hair. "Come a little closer to me, young man. Do not be afraid of me. There is nothing on me that I can harm you with."

"No, I must not move," thought Tall Boy. "I must keep my ground. No I— I must—"

"Come toward me," said the man. "That's it, don't try to fight against my power."

Tall Boy fell to the ground like a dried-up weed. His eyes rolled upward and his entire body stiffened as terror overwhelmed him. He felt the thin line between life and death drawing away from him, and he felt that he was being left inside a black, endless pit. All the beauty of life was lost.

"There," continued the wolf-man as he watched his power work on Tall Boy. "You don't have to worry about your grandfather. All your worries are over and now you can sleep like a small child, at ease." He took out a large black arrowhead from the little bag that hung at his waistline. He felt the edge of the arrowhead to see if it was sharp and he raised it to the sky while his eyes were fastened to the tip of the stone. "People of the night, I ask for your help. With the aid of your power I want to succeed in taking the soul out of this young man who is before me," he said as he stood up.

A strong force engulfed the old man's body and pulled up the heavy bearskin over his shoulder. He let go of the arrowhead and it stood still in midair before it started to turn. His entire surroundings became a dark mist and he saw the image of the young man appear within the turning arrowhead. He felt the enormous power of a bear as he reached for the twirling arrowhead, and the deep groan of a bear rose from his throat. His hand grasped the stone and the energy ran through his body. He bent down and turned the young man's head sideways, cut a handful of his hair at the nape, and wrapped it around the sharp stone. He dipped his left hand into the small pouch and sprinkled a white substance over the young man's body. He returned the arrowhead with the hair to the pouch that contained the powder. He tied up the front of the skin and covered his head with the huge bear-head, and stood on all fours like a bear. He gazed through the eye-holes and visualized the long slow death of the young man.

"Oh, great brown bear of the high mountain," prayed the wolf-man with fury, "with the great strength of your power and with the help of the people of the darkness, take the soul of this man. For you are feared anywhere you go. With your power and mine together—"

From out of the deep south valley came a huge thunder-like sound and it came closer and closer.

The wolf-man tried not to show his surprise at the sudden rumbling as he finished his prayer over Tall Boy's body. He felt happy and successful as he turned to the north and disappeared into the thick shrubs.

The rumbling continued.

II

A gigantic cloud of dust rose like a pillar against the clear sky and came closer and closer. The rumbling became louder and louder, and soon a whole herd of antelope appeared. An enormous buck led the herd out of the rolling hills and down into the wash. They all appeared on the other side and continued onward into the forest.

Hastiin Nizaadi came upon a large hill just as the herd of the antelope passed him. He looked into the thick cloud of dust to see what startled the whole herd of the prairieland antelope. In the south, *Tsoodził,* the turquoise mountain, rose against the sky behind the rising dust. When he did not see anything running after the antelope, he continued to walk home.

His dark brown eyes took in all the beautiful landscape that was before him. The tiny bright flowers stood among the sagebrush and cedar trees. He filled his lungs with sweet fragrances of the damp Mother Earth. Every now and then he reached out and grabbed a handful of cedar leaves or sagebrush. He chewed the leaves, ignoring the bitter taste, and kept walking.

"It sure is odd," thought Hastiin Nizaadi as he gazed into the sky, "for these antelope to be racing at this time of day. On the other hand, those animals may have been stretching their long limbs for the day, in case a bobcat tries to capture one of their newborns. What's that up there? A hawk? No, a crow! But that's too high for any crow to be flying way up there. It looks like it's got a white tail. . . . That is a bald eagle. He must have seen a rabbit below. He is circling over those sagebrush. I hope the bird didn't see me."

Very quickly he sat down behind a small cedar tree and peered at the proud bird. It came down a little closer to the ground. The eagle disappeared among the brush and reappeared out of the cloud of dust, and took the animal. He heard the small rabbit cry and they vanished into the thin air. Silence replaced the noise for awhile. He watch the eagle disappear to the south before he stood up and walked over to where it caught its prey.

Hastiin Nizaadi saw the marks of where the rabbit struggled for its dear life. He looked around to see if the eagle had dropped a feather or two. As he turned around he noticed he was near an edge of a wide wash bed and he walked around for awhile before he heard a low murmur. He peered over the shrub and was astonished.

"Ashkii!" yelled Hastiin Nizaadi as he stumbled down to the bottom, and he became speechless for couple of seconds, but soon regained control. He searched his nephew's body for any cuts or blood. Tall Boy's tongue was slowly turning blue and his whole body stiffened every now and then. His body moved upward as though someone was trying to lift him by his hairless chest. His entire body was covered with sand and his fingers dug into the sand as though grasping for something to hold on to. Hastiin Nizaadi knew at once why his nephew was struggling so helplessly on the sand.

He opened the small bag that hung at his back and took out a tiny pouch that contained the eagle gall. He put a small amount of it into the young man's mouth.

"You will be all right, nephew," Hastiin Nizaadi said, looking around to see where he dropped the skin bag he had filled up with the mountain water. He saw it lying beside a bush and unwrapped the top and poured a small amount of it into his nephew's mouth. He lifted him onto his knee before he washed the dirt from his face. "Wash down the gall powder with this water, nephew. You will be all right—soon." Very gently he slapped him on both cheeks. He looked around to see if there were any tracks of the man-wolf and in which direction it had taken off.

Very gently, he lay his nephew down and pushed his hair off his face. He broke off a thick branch of the nearest sagebrush and brushed the dirt off Tall Boy's body. He chewed a handful of the sagebrush in spite of the bitter taste it gave his mouth and rubbed it onto the young man's face.

"The eagle gall should make him throw up to get rid of the powder the wicked person put on him," he thought. "I'll give him a little bit more water and help him wash it down. I wonder if my father is coming up the trail looking for his—"

At that instant he heard his father.

"Where are you, Ashkii?" bellowed the old man from a hilltop. "You should have been home—"

"Father, he is over here!" yelled Hastiin Nizaadi as he stood above the thick shrubs. He looked toward the north, over the hills that were covered with cedar trees. He wondered if they were the only ones there at the bottom of the valley.

"What happened to your nephew?" asked the old man from a distance.

"Tall Boy has met one of those dried-up feet creatures," Hastiin Nizaadi said, applying some more chewed sagebrush to his nephew's face. "I gave him some of the gall medicine. He should throw up so—"

Before he could finish, the young man's body reacted to the medicine. His stomach pulled itself inwards a couple of times and his fingers dug deeper into the sand.

"Quickly! Turn his head sideways," the grandfather said as he got up and picked up the water bag.

"Grandfather! Don't let go of my hand!" yelled the boy after he threw up and his whole body shook.

"Here, quickly, get him up on his hands and knees. He's probably weak, so hold him up for a while and let him throw up some more." said Hastiin Tabaaha to his son. He was pleased his grandson reacted to the gall medicine. "Don't worry, grandson, I'm here and your uncle is, too. You will be all right, now. We are going to take you home where you will be safe."

"We are here with you, nephew," repeated the young uncle as he brushed the rest of the sand off the boy's back. "Can you hear me? We are here."

"Get him over your shoulder and take him home. I will get the water and hunting bags," the old man said. "We need to get him some lightning herbs and anoint his entire body. We have to help him regain his consciousness in order for him to tell us who he met today."

III

"We anointed his entire body with the lightning herbs," said Hastiin Tabaaha to his visitor.

"How long did it take your grandson to remember who he met, or did he not recognize the person at all?" asked Hastiin Neez, the medicine man. He had coal-black hair even though he was at least seventy winters old.

"It took him a while. Every now and then he became unconscious, but we worked quickly before we let go of him too long." Hastiin Tabaaha drank the rest of the bitter "gameway" plant juice from a gourd spoon. "Yes, he did recognize the old man. I think he is around our age. He's the man with the sharp cutting tongue who expresses his opinion at any time."

The wind rattled the stovepipe and the men glanced up at the moving pipe. A long silence followed.

"Yooch'iid chii'tsoh (Big Fat Liar)," answered Hastiin Nizaadi. "I met him only a couple of times. He is one person I don't want to be around at all."

Hastiin Tabaaha continued, "The only reason why Yooch'iid chii'tsoh speaks out so much is because of his knowledge of witchcraft. He can use it against anyone who puts him down in front of people. My grandson has seen him only twice. Once was at his aunt's wedding and the other time was when a close relative of Yooch'iid chii'tsoh's came back from the Utes. The family had a ceremony for the young woman and they invited us."

"I've watched Yooch'iid chii'tsoh mature into his manhood. Our families were very close but not any more. I heard what happened between your father and him. But I want to hear it from you to see if it really did happen the way I heard from other people," said Hastiin Neez as he looked at the clear blue sky and wondered if it would rain later in the evening.

"Yooch'iid chii'tsoh always bellowed at large gatherings, but he is one of the best orators we have around. He has a deep voice and people listen to him when he speaks out for good cause. Anyway, we were at this huge gathering and he wanted someone to challenge his younger son in a long foot race. He told everyone who was present that no one could beat his son," said Hastiin Tabaaha as he stirred the bright red embers and watched the sparks fly toward the smoke hole. "My father was a good long distance runner back in those days. He used to race me into the foothills every morning up until a couple of moons ago. So my father challenged him in the foot race. The race took place the same day, but Yooch'iid chii'tsoh wanted it to be at his home. However, my father and the people wanted the race the same day."

"I'm surprised the people agreed to have the race right there," said Hastiin Neez as he brought his knees to his chest. "Whenever he shows up people tend to walk away because they don't want to disagree with the man."

"Maybe the crowd as a whole was not afraid of him," continued Hastiin Tabaaha. "Everything was set for the race to start, when Yooch'iid chii'tsoh wanted to change the racing plan. He intended to make the race difficult for my father and a lot easier for his son, but my father immediately said 'no' to the new plan."

"That sounds just like him. I guess he has not changed at all," said Hastiin Neez.

"The men were running side by side near the finish line when his son sprained his ankle, and before he fell on his side, he grabbed for my father's breechcloth. He almost pulled it off. But my father held on to it to the finish line."

"I bet Yooch'iid chii'tsoh went up in flame."

"He sure did, and he tried to make all kinds of excuses for his son. He blames practically everybody but himself," said Hastiin Tabaaha. "To this day he has never spoken to any of my relatives. He has been after us, trying to wipe my whole family off of the earth."

"So far he has not succeeded in his plan," said the medicine man. "Tall Boy was lucky that morning when the antelope startled the man-wolf. If those antelope hadn't appeared at that moment, your grandson's head would now be hanging in the cave of the evil spirit. There is a place where all of the wolf-people meet when they are in need of support from each other."

"Have you been there?" asked Hastiin Tabaaha, trying not to sound so surprised.

"Ah," replied the older man. "Yes, I've been to their meeting place—twice, in fact. But it took us a very long time to find a night when none of the wolf-people were guarding the cave."

▼ ▼ ▼ ▼ ▼ ▼

RAIL

A. A. Hedge Coke

snow on the coal
car white on
black, brown,
red and orange-yellow
steel forged for
rail the box
cars' siding
walls cross
intersection pass
Cerrillos and St. Fran
reading signs
translating message
between lines
courage, mystique
Union Pacific
Sante Fe Southern
rail road
sound resounds
echoes clang
bangs jarring
abrupt clamoring
wheels slide
steel bar wooden
beam laced with
creosote you cannot
burn for wood no matter
how cold you become in
winter the fumes'
noxious choke breath
away at night on
unfamiliar and ignorant
mighty immense

rail   laid into
track   supporting cars,
boxes, passengers, freight
trains   ancient photographs
document paintings
Taos Peoples
advertise Sante Fe
Rail   home to
Southwestern Indians
to Cowboys
to Spaniards
to rich white, white
Anglos   including
Georgia O'Keeffe
or was that
Kit Carson
selling off those
so personal intricate
pieces of art and
artworks   jewelry
traditional clothing
on the plaza   walks
hanging over a clothing
rail   iron rack suspending
works and wares
above cloths, blankets, rugs
under display
earthen ware
tender silver pieces
no not silver,   greenbacks
representing gold
supposedly in mints
from mines supported by
rail   from long, long ago
riding by those
incredible beasts and creatures
frozen   or turned to dust
and stone   in another time

those that the anthros
think formations
they watch with great
no, enormous
humor   they stare at the
rail   being ridden by
so   so   many for so long now
waiting patiently   knowing
all will pass   as did they
in the exact measure
designated span length
bridging rivers   with vast
rich flowing, raging histories
succumbed to dust
arroyos   and such ravines
playing havoc on the telepathic
sensory perceptions
relaying focus to
perspective   in pointillistic
existence   waters remain
unscathed away from the effects
on the environment from the
rail   ever moving onward
ever in repair and   renewal
directions   four cardinal point
ambush   on beauty
not so very distant from here
where we observe this
masterpiece in steel composition
harboring ghost
hobos from eras all but dim
in view   recent recollection
practice   losing legs to catch a
rail   near the New Mexico
School for the Deaf
crosswalk   where
sculptures intrigue a better
answer to *The End of the Trail*

showing rather an Indian man
raising his hands high
including buffalo skull
in prayer his horse
following the preliminary
works' show of defeat
however hope
overrides defeat always
somehow even here with
ear to ground in center
Sante Fe even here
hope is here on this
lonesome familiar
almost outdated
yet never defeated
rail

▼ ▼ ▼ ▼ ▼ ▼

Two Eagles

Heather Ahtone

My uncle said he saw the eagles—two—fly overhead as he prayed to the Creator. I didn't see them, but then I wasn't looking up. I could only see the blood tracing stains on the breasts of the dancers—eyes closed to the sun. My hands trembled against the stillness of my thousand-year-old will passed down by the ghost of my ancestors to this moment—two years ago.

My urbanized eyes—so used to the bloodshed common in the city of angels—begged me to turn away, but were held in place by a spirit surfacing at the call of the drum. Blood pulsating from pride kept rhythm with the left step. Dancers whistled their vision to a sky listening with a clear face.

The holy man approached—I wanted him to stop—recognized me from a battle fought before the white men came. Holding my head high with soft eyes, I watched him pass by without a glance. My eyes dropped, unable to look at the children waiting for birth. Prayers for the elders who could no longer dance for themselves. I raised my eyes to the sun and offered a prayer. I found myself praying openly with a voice I did not recognize as my own.

I looked in time to see the ropes snap and my uncle fall to the ground. A breath escaped as a rush of humility engulfed me. I stepped away from the arbor and walked to the empty field of sage. These were my people—I was one learning to speak to our Creator for the first time. I looked on the horizon with fresh eyes and a fresh spirit and there they were—two eagles—dancing.

Ten Rounds

Lorenzo Baca

TO THE EARTH DOES NOT BELONG TO MAN BELONGS

MOTHER EARTH IS OUR

FALL IS THE TIME OF THE SUN WHEN ALL EARTH MAKES LEAVES

SPRING IS THE TIME OF THE SUN WHEN ALL EARTH MAKES LIFE

THE SNOWS OF WINTER MAKES US PRAY TO SEE

FOR RAIN ON SUMMER AFTERNOONS BRING PRAYERS

ART IMITATES LIFE AS

LIFE IMITATES ART AS

THE DREAM OF PEACE IS

PEACE IS THE LOVE FOR

▼ ▼ ▼ ▼ ▼ ▼

All That Glitters Is Not Gold

(A Fable of Hacienda Galisteo)

Nancy C. Maryboy

In a certain corner of New Mexico, there is a heartbreaking quality of lightness, of translucent blue sky, stretching wide in all directions. It completely dominates all other visible forms. Raven flies through that light, picking up flat gleams that attach to his colorblack feathers. Reflecting back as shine, he glides on that air, heavy, yet floating without effort through the brightness that makes things seem abstract and achingly real at the same time.

Here present melts into past. Lives intertwine in a kind of synchronicity, totally independent of any mortal belief system.

Huge cottonwood trees dot the otherwise empty landscape; some carry more age than two hundred years. They suck up water at an alarming rate, providing shade and lifesaving coolness. Neither sun nor wind show any mercy in this land.

Covered by dirt that sustains the great trees, lay the bones of countless unnamed prehistoric peoples, and of Tanoan peoples, Comanche warriors, Spanish soldiers, Mexican landholders, Anglo farmers, poets, and dreamers. Their stories are the leaves of the trees, waving bright green in spring and dusty dark in fall.

Crumbling adobe buildings stand in picturesque harmony with these giant trees. The mud-baked buildings hold ancient secrets within foot-thick walls. Fresh paint leaves no surface trace of their antiquity. But knock a hole in one and treasures will appear: stone-chipped rock from prehistoric kivas, iron tips from Spanish axes, silver forks from El Patron's kitchen. What is here can be felt best in the early morning light and during the long stillness of night.

Comanche Gap guards the valley from the southwest. A long ridge of black rock runs along the ground, giving way to a pass, a secret entrance for those who wish to remain unseen. Centuries of rock art cover the dark loose boulders. From the top of the ridge Albuquerque can be seen, over fifty miles away. The land, now held as private ranches, is very much the way it looked in 1541. Maybe there was more sagebrush then.

Centuries ago, small groups of people drifted in from the south and north Rio Grande, following prehistoric trails. Joining together, they built seven pueblos that shone golden in the setting sun. Today only Spanish names with scattered building-stones remain: Blanco, Chay, Galisteo, Largo, San Christobal, San Lazaro, and

San Marco. Little remains of Galisteo Pueblo. The hillside that was once home to hundreds now holds only a few isolated homes. Sometimes, though, the spring wind carries hushed voices speaking a soft Tanoan dialect.

T'anu shifted imperceptibly on the rough stone bench. He hoped that his uncle would not notice his restlessness. He was thankful to be inside the coolness of the kiva, sheltered from the hot summer wind that was sucking the moisture from the land. The wind was able to pull the moisture right out of his own body, through the small pores of his skin, through the cracked lips of his mouth. It was because of Wind that the Feathered Serpent clan held this extraordinary midsummer meeting.

T'anu himself should not have been initiated for two more seasons. Yet here he had sat all night and all day, with other boys his own age of thirteen winters. The clan uncles had listened to the oldest men and decided to change the order of things. There was an aura of dry fear, particularly among the elders, for they were now the guardians of Memory. It reminded them of a terrible time, nine generations back, when Wind ran off with Rain and held him captive deep within the Earth.

In those days, Wind blew and blew, puffing out his own importance, while priests prayed to no avail. Women tore their hair and sobbed while brittle-boned babies died of hunger, as shrunk-up breasts hung flaccid, offering no milk, only cracked nipples for listless sucking. Men returned from empty fields carrying withered cornhusks, their faces etched with lines of hunger and despair.

With even their gods deserting them, at last the People walked away from their beautifully constructed cities of stone and headed south. They traveled a lifetime before settling along the Rio Grande, gradually building new pueblos and planting fields of corn.

T'anu's clan was more powerful than others. It was guardian of the sacred mask. No one outside the Feathered Serpent clan ever saw it, but everyone else treated his clan with respect. T'anu had grown up knowing where the bundle was hidden. He was taught to make prayer feathers and he gave corn pollen offerings before he passed four winters. But never had he seen the brightness and power of the sacred mask until last night.

He was ordered to kneel on the red dirt, beside the bench running around the kiva. Fourteen shivering boys, dressed only in breechclouts and fur ruffs, their hair tied with eagle feathers, surrounded him. A One-Horned Kachina with a fierce face painted with a four-pointed star had come down the ladder and danced before the men and boys. The Kachina was carrying the sacred bundle.

T'anu's uncle had beaten the drum while the Red Hawk Priest had sung.

"First Man emerged from a quivering hole of mud," he began. "He danced to life to the beat of his own heart. From the emergence he knew the rhythm of life. He knew the connection between his spirit and his body was the true rhythm of life. He began to sing to the rhythm and put words to his song."

The Red Hawk Priest stopped singing but the drum beat continued. The Serpent Guardian began to sing. He sang of faraway cities of long ago, where buildings shone like the midday sun, blinding one's sight.

The boys were mesmerized. Stiff knees were forgotten as they listened to the songs of these cities far to the south. They saw pyramid-shaped buildings and fierce warrior priests drinking blood from still-beating hearts. They saw noblemen strong and tall dressed in yellow metal that gleamed in sun or moonlight. They saw a gambling fever overtake these proud warriors and the last great gambler shot to the moon on an arrow of light. They listened raptly to the ancient prophecies. Bloodshed and tragedy would follow that yellow metal, streets would run with blood, and the Gods, Morning Star and Feathered Serpent, would be vanquished, even banished from the land. They learned that a pale-skinned warrior race would conquer them and destroy the land. And that one of the pale warriors would be the Great Gambler himself, returning from the heavens with gifts from the moon: four-legged animals to ride and small woolly animals to eat and use for clothing.

The Priests finished and a hush fell over the kiva. Slowly, reverently, the One-Horned Kachina began to unroll the sacred bundle. T'anu's eyes were fixed on the buckskin. It revealed the face of a man. But what a man! He had eyes of sky blue, of turquoise, a rare stone that his uncles dug out of a mine near the north mountains. But they were not the blue of the Pueblo. They were brilliant sky blue, darkened as just before a summer rain. The face of the mask was a gleaming yellow metal. Firelight danced on its cheeks and forehead, sending glints onto the brown faces of all the boys. T'anu thought it was like looking into a pool of water as small breezes riffled the surface. Dancing lights sparkled in all directions.

T'anu couldn't help himself. He gasped with astonishment, then clenched his fists as he saw his uncle glance at him with a reproving look. He was initiated now. He must contain his feelings. No longer could he act as a child, running and laughing with his small sister. He was a full member of Feathered Serpent Clan, Guardians of the Mask.

Two days later the prophecy came true, just as the Priests had predicted. With a sense of foreboding, T'anu had seen the point watchers run back from the mountains of the south.

"Men are coming," they had breathlessly reported to the elders. "They are coming just as it was said. They are riding four-legged creatures and their skin shines as silver."

The boys had crowded around the messengers, squinting against the sun rays and trying to keep the dancing dust out of their mouths. Hot winds swirled around them. The elders were discussing whether to fight or to hide.

T'anu's uncle was grave. He was the principal guardian of the sacred bundle. T'anu was his heir. "Come, Son," he said. "It is time for you to become a man." He led T'anu down into the dim kiva. Dust rose from their footprints as they stepped across the floor. It lingered in the air surrounding the ladder, dust motes glinting darkly through the filtered sunlight.

T'anu's uncle pulled up a large chipped stone near the north wall. He pulled out the well-wrapped bundle and placed it in his nephew's hands. He looked hard at T'anu and spoke with gravity.

"You must run to the mountains of the north and guard the sacred mask. Take your sister with you. Do not return until the leaves have fallen from the picetl tree, and then only with care. I bless you and pray that you go with the protection of the Feathered Serpent."

There was no time for questions. The two quickly ascended the ladder into a square filled with shouts and confusion. The wind was stronger and dust swirled around them. The heat had a feral quality; it smelled of fear, of danger, of death. T'anu ran to his home and found his mother tying a bundle of food for his sister. She added a small pouch of bitter medicine, her most sacred herb. Tears made tracks down her dusty cheeks and her wet eyes shone like stars. She gave each child a fierce hug.

"Go now," she said in a voice just above a whisper. She watched, still as a river stone, until they had run out of sight, her arms clenched around her body as if she still held her babies.

The two children ran fast, as they had been trained. Only once did they stop, on the top of the hill. As they looked back, what they saw filled them with desperate fear. A long dark line of men riding four-legged beasts twisted all the way from the hogback ridge to the pueblo. They were many. Dressed in silver, shining in the sun, so bright that it was hard to look at them, they carried bright flags and made a muted clanking noise. There were more of these men than in the entire pueblo. The children looked at each other with awe, then turned and ran north.

T'anu and his sister knew they should remain in the mountains until the picetl tree lost their leaves. They were protectors of a sacred trust. For forty days they lived among the forest animals, under trees of quaking green leaves, beside silvery streams. They prayed for guidance. They sang the songs of their grandfathers. They made prayer feathers and gave offerings. They continued to wander through the mountains.

One day they came to a dark wall with many carvings. T'anu saw a large spiral figure in the center of many hands. He understood the meaning. It spoke of the countless migrations of his people, of birth and rebirth, of stability but always with change. Somehow even in the midst of change, some things stayed constant. There was eternal return. One life meant little, survival of the people meant everything. Next to the spiral he saw a feathered water serpent. "This is my clan," he marveled. Then he saw two warriors with the faces of stars, outstretched eagle claws and fanned tail feathers. "The Warrior Twins," he told his sister.

Soon the slender picetl trees began to shed their pointed leaves. The children knew it was time to return to the village.

Carefully they made their way through the mountains. It was a cold afternoon when they reached the hill near the Pueblo. The sky had a yellow light. There was absolutely no sound. The wind had disappeared. It was deathly quiet as it was quiet death. Skeletal bodies lay piled up in a corner. Bows and arrows were carelessly scattered around. Not a dog or turkey moved. A fine film of red dust covered everything and everyone. There was no firesmoke, no children's cries, no low chanting coming from the underground kivas.

T'anu and his sister ran to their mother's house. Every carefully painted pot was smashed. Orange and red shards were everywhere. Colored kernels of dried corn and small dark beans were scattered over the floor. They stood still, remembering their mother's concern that everything be in its right place.

T'anu went to the kiva. The door covering was gone. He descended the ladder, not daring to breathe. As his eyes grew accustomed to the dimness he saw that all the handworked stones were overturned. Sacred feathers were scattered. Powders and pigments were jumbled together on the kiva floor. Gourd rattles were smashed and tiny rivers of black onyx and red garnets mingled on the dust floor.

He backed up in horror, then started as his foot brushed against something brittle. He gasped as he recognized the headdress of the One Horned Priest. An outstretched bony hand had brushed against the boy's ankle. The headdress was askew, a long crack ran the length of his skull. A sharp lance stuck out from his chest. One hand grasped the shaft of the lance, the other was thrown across eyeless sockets, as if to cover them from the desecration.

T'anu screamed and scrambled blindly up the ladder. He and his sister met, shaking, in the plaza. They did not dare look closely at the pile of bodies. They could not speak. They clung to each other, sobbing, mouths open, without a sound.

Years later, when Chama was a very old woman, she recounted the horror of that night.

"When I was small we had been happy. The soil along the river was good. The hunting in the mountains was fine. We were seldom hungry. Our men worked a turquoise mine near the east mountains. The village was prosperous. Then things began to change. The wind began again and slowly the land lost all moisture. That was when the Spanish came. We knew they were coming from the prophecies of our grandfathers. And so they came."

She paused to pick a kernel of corn from an aching hollow in a back tooth. A grandchild named Fernando snuggled closer to her side.

"That night we returned, T'anu and me. We returned to a pueblo of death. The moon came up and found us sleeping where the grain had been stored. We curled into each other. It was the only security we had left. All else had been taken from us. My brother still guarded the sacred bundle. I had nothing."

The old lady rubbed her eyes, as if Memory made her see the scene once again clearly.

"Just as the moon was finishing its travels of the night and was ready to lie down in the west, they came." She paused.

"Around the corner they came, and they were upon us before we knew enough to be awake. I don't know where they came from. I heard shouts in a language I could not understand. I saw shining metal glinting in the last moonlight. My brother jumped up and fought bravely, like a warrior. But he could not outfight four of them, with their metal weapons. He still had the sacred bundle. I saw him pull out the wrapped buckskin, hold it high over his head for a moment, then throw it as far as he could. I remember how it sailed over the low wall into the field below. Then one of the men shouted and ran his sword straight through my brother's neck. Blood spurted out and he fell backwards. I thought of the Feathered Serpent as the blood ran over the top of his head and fanned out behind him."

Again the old lady paused. Her wide-eyed grandchildren had heard the story before but each time they dared hope that it would turn out different. Fernando gave a long sigh.

"I screamed and began to run. A man with a bearded face ran after me and caught me at the place where we ground corn. He held me by the hair and shoulders. He gave a crazy laugh, then pulled me back to the others. They threw me down in the dirt next to my brother and pulled my skirt over my head. I tossed my head from side to side as the blood of my brother slowly soaked through my skirt and down onto my closed eyes."

She paused and stared far off into the distance. The small grandson whimpered and she pulled him closer. The firelight showed glimmers of tears in the old woman's eyes.

"Well, my children, they had their way with me. And I wasn't even eleven winters. They took me away with them the next day, tied to a mule, roped to the bearded one's horse. They knew I would try to run away or kill myself, and I did try, over and over. But they watched me with the eyes of hawks, and I never got away. I can still feel the shame of it."

The old woman sighed, feeling very old and heavy with emotion. She had been the only survivor of an entire pueblo. These part-Spanish grandchildren would be the next guardians of the Memory.

"They took me far to the south. I learned their language and in time I had nine children. All of you are part Spanish, but you are also of the Pueblo."

One boy, braver than the rest, straightened up and asked his great-grandmother the question that had been haunting him all night.

"But what about the mask?" he asked, "What happened to the golden mask?"

The very old woman looked hard at the young boy. He felt her dark eyes pierce deep inside him.

"It lay where my brother threw it. It is still there, covered by Mother Earth, still in the field, over the wall."

She continued to stare at the boy, who didn't dare move.

"It came from the south. It is a very dangerous thing. It is called *oro* and it is not for us."

Years passed. The very old grandmother died and others took her place. The merciless sun continued to rise and set. The blue sky with unbearable lightness continued to stare down, as many people came and left.

Other Spaniards came, priests with rough robes wearing small crosses around their necks, crosses of men hanging with hands nailed fast and bloody to the wood. Soldiers traveled through the land, killing those who dared believe that the People's gods were more powerful than their God.

One year the People revolted, killing off many Spaniards. Some years later, when they learned that the Spanish soldiers were returning to exact a harsh revenge, the

People left, traveling far to the north, to join with other tribes, forming new clans.

The few people who remained were as hostages in their own land. The sun shone down on terrible scenes of bloodshed, rapes, and slavery. Comanches came raiding through the gap. The fierce warriors on feathered horses showed no mercy. The Pueblo became deserted.

Later, still more Spaniards came. They built small adobe forts, cross-topped churches, finally grand haciendas.

Don Juan Ortiz y Rosa was born in one of these haciendas. He was the grandson of a Spanish soldier, and he had raped an Indian girl as she was returning from the waterhole carrying a large *olla* on her head. She was only thirteen and should have been married the next year. But Don Ortiz y Rosa, who himself was only seventeen, saw her beauty and could not control himself. After the rape he had her moved into the hacienda as third kitchen assistant and so she grew to adulthood in the house, suffering his frequent assaults. The Indian girl, shamed and grieving, put a curse on the Patron. Her baby son grew up in the household, looking more like the Patron than like his mother. When Don Ortiz y Rosa discovered that he could not father more children, he grew fond of Pedro and insisted that the bastard be raised as a Spaniard and educated as his lawful son. The Indian girl was sent away and not heard from again.

Pedro grew up ashamed of his Indian ancestry. He became known as Don Pedro, a fair and respected Patron. He married Doña Carmelita Peron, herself a product of Indian rape, several generations removed. They had no sons, to their sorrow, but three daughters brought them joy.

Luz de Ciel was the youngest. She was named after the clear blue sky framing the hacienda. While the elder daughters were dutiful, quiet, well-behaved young Spanish ladies, Luz de Ciel was unruly, from her dark, curly hair to her willful ways. She loved to ride her horses over the prairies for hours, frightening her mother, who worried constantly about Comanche raids. She loved to talk to the Indian women in the kitchen about herbs, healing, and affairs of the spirit. She gave Don Pedro the greatest concern, and she also gave him the most joy. Light of the sky, he couldn't bear to think of losing her.

The eldest two daughters married at an early age and disappeared with stiffly bearded husbands to Santa Fe. Luz stayed home, becoming wilder.

"No one will want her," despaired Doña Carmelita, shaking her head and disappearing into the coolness of the church across the road to pray for her wayward daughter. Don Pedro agreed, but he couldn't imagine Luz de Ciel leaving the land that she loved.

One day, during a cold and windy winter, a young man rode up, shivering and alone. Peter Sebastian was the first American to appear in Galisteo. He almost fell off his horse at their gate, and he stumbled into the hacienda more dead than alive. Doña Carmelita put him to bed at once and he lay there for ten days as a fever raged within his body. Luz de Ciel became his healer after arguing with her mother over choices of herbs. In the end, she placed poultices of a very bitter medicine, chimaja, on his feverish forehead while he twisted and turned, shook and chilled and burned. As she had known, the chimaja calmed him, and he began to recover. Long days passed as the weakened man built up his strength and told his stories to the fascinated girl. He was not immune to her dark beauty, and as the days went by he fell deeply in love.

Sebastian did not know how things were done in New Mexico. He was a wealthy artist who accompanied an army expedition just after the American government had acquired an enormous tract of the Southwest. He stayed back to investigate the ruins of an abandoned pueblo and became immersed in his sketching. When he tried to find the regiment, it had disappeared and he caught the fever the second night alone, when he had slept at the head of a canyon.

"I love you and want to marry you," he told her. Luz de Ciel was thrilled. He could stay here and run the hacienda with Papa. She too could stay here and continue her life of herbs and healing. She didn't really love Sebastian, but she was fascinated by his stories and by the certain knowledge that marrying him would ensure her life at the hacienda that she loved.

"You must ask my father," she replied, primly folding her hands over her lap, gazing out the window to the far prairies where her heart belonged. "You will have to pay the bride price."

Peter Sebastian came from a wealthy Charleston family. Six months later he came riding through the courtyard of the hacienda. He dismounted from a fine red stallion and walked inside. There he placed a green embroidered silk bag filled with gold coins on the gleaming dark table that had been carved in Spain over one hundred years ago. With that bag of gold coins he bought the hacienda as well as Luz de Ciel.

She had been waiting expectantly for Sebastian's return. But the very moment that he opened the bag of gold coins, a shadow crossed her face as the glittering coins tumbled onto the table. She remembered an old story of her grandmother's, passed down by Don Pedro. She was surprised to remember this, because her father seldom spoke of his Indian mother. She could not remember the story, but she felt revulsion toward the shiny coins. She also had a premonition of danger. The young couple married in the cathedral of Santa Fe, with a very grand ceremony. A year later, they had one son, but shortly thereafter Luz de Ciel moved across the courtyard into the small adobe room that had been her Indian grandmother's.

As the years went by she spent more and more time in that room, emerging only for horseback rides over the prairie or to gather herbs along the clear stream that bubbled past the hacienda. She was heard late at night conversing with her long-passed grandmother. Adults became increasingly afraid of her, yet village children had no fear of the tall dark woman with unruly hair. She never argued with her husband, often eating dinner with him under the large cottonwood tree in the courtyard. After dinner she gave him a gentle smile and returned to her room.

One hot, still afternoon, Peter Sebastian fell off his horse and died. He was only thirty years old. He was buried in the churchyard in the section reserved for non-Catholics. Luz de Ciel remained in her small room, while her young son, Ramon Sebastian, took over his father's quarters in the big house. Don Ramon never married, much to the dismay of several mothers of girls of marriageable age. He was kind and even-tempered, running the hacienda with a fair hand and prospering mightily. Mother and son grew old together. They shared a fascination for herbs, healing, and early morning walks, and they adored the special quality of light that surrounded them.

Luz de Ciel died in her sleep the night she became one hundred years old. Towards the end of her life she could scarcely remember her husband but still spoke every night with her grandmother. Ramon was distraught. He decided to leave the hacienda and spend his remaining years in travel. It was common knowledge that he desired to sell the hacienda.

A young American artist named Andrew West came from Oregon and befriended Luz de Ciel just ten months before she died. Andrew spent hours talking to the old woman, sitting by her bed, and supporting her arm as they walked slowly by the stream. He came to know old Indian stories, Spanish tales, herbal lore, and healing techniques. He was quiet and he listened well.

One spring afternoon they watched from the shade of the large cottonwood as a fine-boned American woman drove up in a bottle-green Jaguar. They watched her go inside the old adobe house to speak with Don Ramon. She came out, her face aglow with excitement. Expensive rings glittered as she opened the door and slid back into the car. The top of the convertible was down, and she seemed to laugh as she gunned the motor, racing out of the driveway, spewing up small pebbles and scaring the finches.

"She wants to buy the hacienda," announced Don Ramon that evening as the three of them sat under the cool shade of the ancient cottonwood tree, sipping icy cold *limonadas*. The old woman did not say a word, pulling her flowered shawl closer around her thin neck.

"Who is she?" asked Andrew, feeling a chill that could not have come from the soft spring breeze.

"Her name is Crystal White," answered Don Ramon, puffing on his pipe. "She runs the Institute of Spiritual Light in Santa Fe."

There was a long pause. Still the old woman said nothing.

"She calls it New Age Spiritual Progress, and she told me she facilitates the dreams of clients. It is very expensive to be facilitated. Many people come to study with her. She charges large sums."

The icy *limonada* stung Andrew's throat. He began to shiver. Luz de Ciel said only one word in her ancient, quavering voice: "Rubbish."

Shortly after the old woman's death, the green Jaguar again pulled up to the hacienda. That morning Andrew West set up an easel and began sketching the old church from the hillside. He watched the woman get out of the car. She was dressed completely in white, with a turban wrapped around her head. In her hands she carried a buckskin bag richly decorated with cut glass beads and seashells. It looked heavy. He suddenly felt too depressed to continue his sketching. He stood up and began to walk back to his house.

When he reached home he was startled to find an unusual green plant had budded out and was running all along the base of his house. The leaves looked like wild parsley, curled and large. This must be the bitter chimaja herb, he thought. Luz de Ciel had mentioned its almost magical qualities, but he had never seen it before.

"But she is gone," he said to himself, overcome by the loss of his companion. Suddenly he began to pick the chimaja, stuffing it into a large basket. Around the house he went, picking every leaf until none remained.

Exhausted, he went inside and fell asleep. Very early the next morning he arose and walked up to the hillside where he had left the easel. The sun was not yet up, the dawn felt fresh and clean. He walked over an ancient low crumbling wall, descended the hill, and paused, looking to the south.

He looked towards Comanche Gap, the hole through which centuries of raiders had come. He thought he heard murmurs, then voices. Many voices, indecipherable languages, laced with Spanish and English. He turned his head; perhaps it was only the wind. But the voices came again, insistent. He looked at his feet. Something glimmered at his boot. He reached down, brushed off the red dirt, and picked up a small golden mask. The eyes were a deep blue turquoise, darkened by age, older by far than anything he had ever seen.

Andrew's hands shook. He could not begin to imagine the history of this golden mask that danced shimmering in his hands. It must be ancient. It must be very valuable. "I could sell it. I could buy the hacienda!" he thought. He had a vision of himself as Patron, in a white suit. It must be a white suit and he must have a broad Panama hat. Yet just as quickly came the voice of Luz de Ciel: "No, gold must not buy our land, it brings danger." It had something to do with a dimly remembered legend, one that he couldn't fully recall.

The mask looked Mexican, perhaps Toltec or Aztec. Again he questioned, "How did it get here? How long since anyone has held it in his hand?"

Suddenly, grabbed by an urge he could not explain, he raised the little golden mask and hurled it across the sky. He turned abruptly and never saw where it landed.

That afternoon he took the basket of green chimaja leaves to Don Ramon. He knew the older man was interested in unusual plants. It was a parting gift, for he could not bear to watch the hacienda turn into the Institute of Spiritual Light.

He found his friend in a joyful, expansive mood.

"Oh," thought Andrew, "he's going to tell me that he sold the hacienda to that woman." He felt unbearably sad. With shaking hands, he offered the basket to Don Ramon. He was not prepared for the look of gratitude and love that crossed the face of the older man.

"Andrew," he said. "I am going to tell you a story." Andrew nodded his head in silence as the two men sat down in the cane chairs under the cottonwood tree. Don Ramon ran his fingers through the basket of chimaja as he spoke.

"The rich American returned yesterday. She came to buy the hacienda and carried with her a beaded bag. We had already agreed on a price of a hundred thousand dollars. I thought she would have cash. She opened the bag. It was full of gold coins. I stared at them as they spilled all over my grandfather's table. She just laughed, saying, 'I went all the way to Paris to get these gold coins. Do you have any idea how difficult it is to find gold coins, Don Sebastian? The idea came to me in a dream state. I must pay for the hacienda with the most brilliant of gold coins. The Institute of Spiritual Light must be founded with the shiniest new gold. Of course, it was an expensive trip, but the Institute will make up for it, as soon as we open in the hacienda.' She looked around while running the gold coins through her fingers. 'You will leave the furniture, won't you? I can just see this dear table as the registration desk.'

"I stared at those coins with a feeling of horror. I remembered how Mama had told me the story of the gold coins and how Peter Sebastian had purchased her and the hacienda. Something went wrong with their marriage, and he died when he was only thirty."

Andrew listened with a growing feeling of excitement.

"Andrew, do you know what I told Señorita White?"

"No," murmured the younger man.

"I told her the hacienda was not for sale. She couldn't have it at any price."

Andrew jerked his head up in surprise. He had been holding it between his hands as if it was a fragile melon.

"What?"

"Yes, I told her that the deal was off. Didn't my mother tell you the story of how Peter Sebastian got this place?" Don Ramon always referred to his father in this remote fashion, "Peter Sebastian." He had been close to his mother and rarely spoke of his father.

"Well, yes," remembered Andrew. And he also recalled Luz de Ciel's words as they had come to him that morning on the hill.

The two men, one old, one young, spent the rest of the daylight making plans under the old cottonwood tree. The same tree that had seen so much joy, so much pain. The tree took it all in through its leaves, leaving in return cool shade and peace.

Andrew West was able to buy the hacienda at a greatly reduced price, over time. Don Ramon was able to spend his remaining years in travel, just as he had wished. The sun continued to beat down, showing no mercy, no favorites, and the sky continued to shine with unbearable lightness.

▼ ▼ ▼ ▼ ▼ ▼

Ka Po'o Owenge

Rosemary Diaz

Grandma's flowers wilted,
she left Ka po'o Owenge.*
Seven children and there were no jobs
on the reservation.
Since the tourist had stopped
buying pottery
there was no need to make clay.

They moved to Pomona
where Grandma cleaned house for Sonny:
a withery white woman who
paid her bus fare.

Grandma cleaned house for Sonny
even on cold days
when her hands longed most
for the moist clay.

She returned to Ka po'o Owenge and
planted her flowers again:

the clay was calling her home.

**Original Tewa name for Santa Clara Pueblo, New Mexico. Translates to "village where roses grow next to singing water."*

▼ ▼ ▼ ▼ ▼ ▼

The Crows

Rachael Arviso

It was a cool, crisp day in November. That day Grandma happened to stop at the house on her way home from visiting relatives. Out of courtesy I fixed dinner rather early that day. We lived in a three bedroom house trailer on the outskirts of a rural community in New Mexico.

Justin quickly became bored listening to the same old gossip about his mother's family. He talked about our mare that had just foaled a couple days before. Justin was a rodeo steer wrestler before we were married. After we married, he trained horses. The mare had previously been trained as a steer-wrestling horse and she worked well for awhile. In the steer-wrestling rodeo event, the rider called a "bull dogger" rides by a steer on horseback, going about fifteen to twenty miles an hour. He jumps onto the steer's horns and wrestles the steer down until all four hooves are pointed in one direction. The mare did great for the first couple of runs, but she began carrying the rider too wide. Then she got to a point where she wouldn't run by the steers so we had to look for another horse. The horse was then bred to an Appaloosa stud. Justin then got his next prized steer-wrestling horse. It was a big bay gelding that had previously gone three times to the Indian National Finals Rodeo. The contestants riding him each time had won the steer-wrestling title. Although it wasn't rodeo time, the horses were the prime activity of the day. We couldn't keep our horses at the trailer park, so they were stabled about eight miles away.

Grandma was anxious to see the new colt the children had named Sissy. After dinner everyone left to see and feed the horses. I stayed home to clean the dishes. As I began washing them, I pictured the children running about trying to catch Sissy. She was a beautiful, leggy sorrel mare. The family would take their time feeding the horses. I busied myself putting clothes in the washing machine. As I checked my little boys' pockets for rocks, a series of loud squawks came from the front door. I thought that some crows were fighting and I continued to fix the clothes to be washed. Again, the same horrible loud noises came. A crow had to be fighting with a dog or cat. The noises were so loud that I thought the front screen might even be open. My hands quickly dropped the pants and I ran down the hall to the front door. The screen door was closed. I looked out the top window on the screen door.

The front door faced east to the driveway. The next couple of trailer lots were empty, so the next trailer was about a block away. Mount Taylor was on the horizon. Our driveway was empty. From where did those noises come? I checked the area on my right, a small tin shed. Nothing was there. We didn't even have a dog or cat. I turned away and the noise sounded again.

Again, I looked out. In the middle of the driveway, a crow hovered in mid-air. It was not going anywhere but it flapped its wings rapidly. It stayed in one place about eight feet above the ground, talking to me.

I panicked. A cold chill ran down my spine. I froze for a moment, or was it longer? I couldn't move. I wondered if I was dreaming.

The screeching noise brought me back. Slowly I opened the door, expecting the crow to fly away. It was very close, about six feet away.

Its screeches were so loud—it was talking. Who was it screeching at? What was it saying? I looked above the door where I now stood to see if was something was there. Nothing was there. The crow really was talking to *me!*

Beautiful, silky, and shiny, it held its weight in mid-air. The black feathers moved, flapping fast, yet it seemed to move in slow motion. Its tongue stuck out as the beak opened and closed. I saw the limbs in the crow's wing. They looked strong. The feathers folded evenly in place as the wings drew downward. Outstretched, the wings seemed to contain many individual fingers.

Time stood still. For a moment, I didn't hear the squawking it made. Then, as if sensing my fear or confusion, it cried even louder. Still hovering in the same spot in mid-air, it defecated. Its droppings were watery.

At that moment, I knew this was not good. I turned immediately and went back inside. I asked myself, "Why did I watch it do that?" Trying to make sense out of the whole ordeal, I answered myself, "How was I to know what it was going to do?" Sitting on the bed, I worried about this strange thing and wondered where everyone was.

Some time later, I returned to the front door. Cautiously, I opened it and walked out. The crow's droppings were on the ground. It really did happen.

Washing dishes and clothes afterward was a blur. As soon as the family returned, I tried to tell Justin, but the children had stories of their own. I pulled Grandma aside to tell her about the crow. She said, "You need to seek aid from a medicine man to interpret this."

Justin was between pay periods. I was not employed and Grandma did not have any money. There was no money to hire a medicine man to correct this situation.

The next four days were frantic. The older children went to school and

Justin went to work. I stayed home. The little boys remained home with me and they kept me busy. Only when everyone was tucked in bed at night did I have time to relax.

When four days passed with nothing drastic happening, I resumed normal duties. But I began to do an odd thing: As I cleaned house, I often stopped to look at my face whenever I passed a mirror. I usually did not wear makeup and seldom did I ever pay attention to my face. Several times though, I caught myself staring into the mirror, at my face. This was not impulse, I was under a spell to do it.

Thanksgiving came. Our family had a huge dinner. Grandma came to visit again. She asked how things were. By then I had already forgotten the crow.

The children were still pretty excited about the new colt. Winter was upon us. We began to build a shelter for the horses. Otherwise, our daily routine was the same. The house was filled with laughter and the sounds of Christmas carols.

Three weeks before Christmas, late one Sunday evening, Justin's brother, John, arrived with his wife, Mae. They stayed for dinner and saw the colt. The Appaloosa stud, the colt's father, belonged to John. He and his wife were pleased at the stud's offspring. John decided to start charging a stud fee after seeing the colt. Before leaving, John invited Justin and me to a Christmas dinner and party in Gallup sponsored by the mine where he worked. We accepted happily.

This was to be a treat for us. It had been a long time since Justin and I had gone out on the town to celebrate. The last time was on our anniversary, back in January.

John and Mae picked us up around seven o'clock Saturday night. We left our older children in charge of the smaller boys. The little ones were already tucked in bed.

On our way to town, John said, "Dinner is free, but the drinks—cocktails—are not." To compensate for what looked like an expensive evening, John pulled out a fifth of Calvert whiskey. Mae mixed drinks as the guys recalled previous winters in their younger days. Mae and I nursed our drinks all the way to town.

Justin and John were pretty merry when we sat down to eat turkey and dressing. We all had one drink with our meal. Dancing began near the dining area. Our table was filled with many familiar faces. Everyone was having a great time, talking at the same time above the music.

We began to dance off our huge dinners. Justin acted like a freshman in high school; he twirled me all around the dance floor. I wasn't able to remember the last time we had danced and laughed so much. After many dances, I was completely exhausted. "I need to rest," I told Justin. John and Mae had sat at the table throughout this entire time, conversing with another couple. John laughed a lot with a coworker while Mae and that fellow's wife talked more seriously.

At midnight, John wanted to go to another place. We left the party; something had happened between John and Mae. Justin sensed tension and we decided to go home.

On the way there, at a small rural community, John stopped at his favorite out-of-the-way bar. The parking lot was crowded. Mae asked John not to stop. "They want to check the kids first," she told John, but to no avail. She knew John would take his time inside. She and I decided to go and use the ladies' rest room. We left Justin outside; he was half asleep anyway. "Dear, are you all right?" I asked. "Mae and I are going to the ladies' room. We'll hurry," I said as we got out of the truck. As an afterthought, I asked, "Hey, do you want to come inside?" He didn't answer. John had already disappeared into the bar.

Inside was very crowded. Mae and I inched our way to the back where the rest rooms were located. A line of people waited there. Since we didn't have a choice, we waited, too. People stopped to talk with Mae. When I finally came out of the ladies room, we inched our way toward the bar entrance again.

There was a ruckus up there. About eight feet from the door, we were stopped. The bar bouncer was stopping everyone from entering and exiting. Justin stood at the entrance as the bouncer pushed everyone in front of us backwards into us. Justin tried to come inside, but the door closed in his face.

People pushed and shoved. The bar was hot, smoky, and smelly. We rocked against each other, swerving from side to side, but still pushing ourselves toward the door. At last we felt some cool air; Mae and I were outside. The wind blew, snow came down. Justin wasn't there.

In the parking area, people yelled, "He stabbed a kid."

"We'll call the police!" a man answered as he ran past, almost knocking me down. Mae turned to me and asked, "Who is he talking about? Do you know him?"

"No," I answered. "Where's Justin?"

"There he is, whose all those guys?" Five white guys stood around John's truck.

"I don't know." I hurried toward the pickup. Justin had his hands on the door handle, trying to open the door. He was barely able to hold himself upright. A stocky white guy with a beard, two times the size of Justin, pushed him toward the rear of the truck. Justin felt his way along the truck to the bumper. Two more white guys immediately surrounded Justin. Another man ran toward the bar.

I reached Justin and asked, "What are they talking about? Did you get in a fight?"

"No! Where in the hell were you? You took too damn long. I tried to find you but they wouldn't let me in the bar. That damn honky bouncer kept pushing me outside. There was a fight in the cars parked by the bar entrance. I guess someone got stabbed!"

"Where's your knife?" I asked. He always carried one.

"In my pocket," he said.

"God, of all the times to have it! Any other time you wouldn't be able to find it," I said sarcastically.

"I didn't do it!" Justin said, looking around. "But do you think these white bastards will believe me?"

"Well, give me the knife," I said.

"I can't get it out, it's in my right pocket," he fumbled at his pocket, trying to hurry. I slipped my hand in his pants pocket and pulled the knife out. I looked at it, not able to think! "What do I do now?" I asked him.

"Get rid of it. Go on!" he whispered, hanging onto the truck.

I turned and left him, walking away from the truck and bar. I didn't know what to do. I couldn't decide where there were more cars. I went back in the direction of the truck. "Mae," I yelled, "Watch Justin."

She answered, "I can't. Where in the hell is John? I need to find him. They might do something to the truck."

She reentered the bar. I was still trying to decide where to put the knife. I went completely around the bar, and decided to put it on the other side. Standing among the cars and trucks, I looked at the knife. The blades were clean. I thought of all the trouble Justin and I went through to find this particular kind of knife.

Justin had always owned a knife ever since he was able to remember. That was the only thing his father made sure Justin had on the ranch, especially when Justin was by himself. Justin's father always owned a good case brand even though they are very hard to find, and they are expensive. I had bought more expensive knives for Justin, but he would not own any other brand. Personally I couldn't see the difference in knives, but he did.

I remembered the day when we finally found that knife. It was after a week-long search, going from store to store all over Albuquerque. Justin really needed a knife, and since he finally had enough money, he decided to get what he wanted. We went to Old Town. In the shop where we had purchased my first genuine leather jacket four years before, Justin knelt at the glass cabinet beneath the cash register. A salesman lifted out a tray of knives. Justin slowly picked out the prettiest one. It was six inches long. It had a brown shiny covering on both sides, with silvery streaks that glared at a certain angle. He slowly opened the knife blades. The two blades were sharp. The longest blade, about five inches in length, almost gleamed. Justin couldn't take his eyes from the knife. The salesman said, "Case knife blades seldom get dull right away." We bought that knife then. Looking at it in the parking lot lights, I decided to keep it.

I had to hide it from them. "Where?" I asked myself as I stood between two trucks, resting my hand on one of them. Beneath me, there was a hole. I could have dropped it down in there, but I decided against it. I looked around again. The bar had a flat roof, similar to a pueblo building. I considered tossing it up there. Then Justin and I could go back and get it later. I decided not to do that either.

Finally I decided to put it in my boot. Balancing myself against the truck, I took off my right boot and placed the knife in my sock. As I put the boot back on again, the knife slipped to the ball of my foot. I couldn't put my full weight on it.

At John's truck, a group of men held Justin against it.

"He did it!" yelled a kid, who wasn't old enough to go in any bar.

"Are you sure? This guy stabbed that kid?" another white guy asked.

"Did someone call the police?"

"What are you saying? Leave him alone!" I screamed running to Justin.

"Get the hell away," shouted someone.

"He didn't do it. Leave him alone," I said, limping on.

"Get that bitch away from here. I'm going to shoot the damn Indian!" A huge guy started to take aim at Justin with a shotgun.

I don't know much about guns, but I knew I was looking at a double-barreled shotgun.

"No, no, leave him alone!" I yelled again.

"He did it! We have witnesses! Get the hell out of here," another man swore at me. They surrounded Justin.

Justin tried to steady himself against the truck. By then I was within a few feet of Justin. The man with the shotgun cocked the barrel. "No! No!" I screamed and dove at him.

The sound of the gun went through the night. Then there was silence. I couldn't hear anything. I knew I went down. Everything was black. I didn't know if my eyes were open. I tried hard to open them.

How long I blacked out I don't know. Something hurt me. That damn honky with the gun had hit me, on the right side of my cheek, with the butt of the shotgun. My face felt huge and numb. As he struck me with the gun, it fired.

Mae was at my side pulling me up. "Where's Justin?" I mumbled.

There was complete confusion. Everyone panicked at the sound of the shotgun. They ran in all directions.

"Man, you better put that gun away," someone yelled.

Another voice added, "Here comes the cops!"

The man with the gun fired again. He shot into the air this time.

Justin was at the truck, at the door on the driver's side. He was coming toward me. I looked around again, wondering where I was. I had fallen by the rear left tire.

Loud sirens and flashing lights were in the distance. The police then used the bullhorn, warning everyone to keep away.

An officer approached the man holding the gun. "Do you have a license for that weapon?" he asked. "Who are you? What were you shooting at?" His questions had only started.

Before the man answered, another said, "Officer, I saw this man stab a kid," and he pointed to Justin.

"Who got stabbed? Where is he?" asked the cop. "Call the ambulance," he added.

"It's on the way," another officer answered. "How badly is he stabbed?"

"Let me see some identification," the first one demanded of the man who fired the gun. "Everyone calm down. Who saw what happened?"

Justin was at my side, "Are you hurt?" I asked.

"No. What about you? Did he shoot you?"

"No. But I hurt," I replied.

John appeared out of nowhere. "What happened?" he asked in the Navajo language.

Mae immediately jumped at him. "Where in the hell have you been?"

John answered her sharply in Navajo.

The police officers approached Justin. "We have to arrest you for the stabbing that occurred tonight."

"He didn't do anything," I said and pushed myself directly in front of Justin.

A second officer approached me. He asked of someone I couldn't see, "This lady?" and pointed at me.

"Yes," a voice answered. I couldn't see my accuser; spotlights glared in my face.

"Are you his wife?" the officer asked.

"Yes," I said. "What are you doing?" I asked as he reached for my elbow. I added, "That man with the shotgun hit me in the face with the butt of the gun."

"How do you know it is a shotgun?" the officer asked me.

"I know. Why aren't you going to arrest *him?*" I asked as I pointed at the man who had struck me.

"He owns the bar. He has a license for that gun," the officer answered.

"I don't care. He tried to shoot my husband for no reason," I challenged.

"I'm sorry, lady, but I'm going to have to arrest you," the officer informed me.

"For what?" I asked, stunned.

"Obstructing a police officer from performing his duties."

"Then arrest him, too!" I yelled.

Other police officers and the owner of the bar were all huddled together nearby.

"Lady, if you don't shut up, I can add more charges like resisting arrest. It's up to you. Turn around, I need to cuff you," he said as he spun me around.

I turned around, trying hard to keep my mouth shut. Am I this dangerous? I wondered. I couldn't see Justin. John and Mae were still arguing. The officer led me to a police car. There was still a mass of commotion as people spilled out of the bar. It was closing time and probably the first time the bar emptied right on time, at two in the morning.

"Watch your head as you get in," the officer warned.

I bent my head as I sat in the back seat of the police car. Justin appeared at the window. "There you are. Are you okay?" I whispered to him as he got inside.

"Yeah. Where did you put the knife?" He wanted to know. "You know none of this would have happened if you didn't go in the bar." Justin was angry. "Where's the knife?" He snapped at me. He turned his whole body to me because his hands were also cuffed behind his back.

I had to think hard to remember. "Oh, it's in my boot."

"What the hell's wrong with you?" he exploded. "I told you to get rid of it!"

"For what? You didn't use it," I answered.

"That doesn't matter. You saw how that guy almost shot you."

I stopped to think. John came to my side of the police car. The window was rolled down about six inches.

Justin and John started talking in Navajo about me. Quickly, I twisted my hands in the cuffs and freed my right hand. I had always wondered if that was possible. I only saw it in the movies. It took a couple of minutes. The metal scraped my fist. It hurt and I almost gave up the idea, but I didn't. With my free hand I pulled my boot off again and took out the knife. Just as John pulled it through the window and before he could hide it, a police officer saw us. Right away he yelled for assistance. Other cops dashed at us. They took the knife from John and arrested him right there, too. They placed John in the same police car with us. I sat in the middle between Justin and John, still holding my hands behind me as if they were still cuffed.

The twenty-mile trip to town was quiet. In that time, I squeezed my hand back into the handcuffs. Justin slept for awhile. Walking into the jail, he kept asking me what had happened. My head throbbed from the pain; I didn't feel like explaining. John was so mad that he didn't talk. We were all booked into jail. I couldn't believe it. I had never been incarcerated. The police took all our possessions.

"I need to go to the hospital," I told the officers. They wouldn't listen. As the cell door closed, one officer said that as soon as things got quiet for them they would take me to see a doctor. They were busy locking up the usual drunks.

In the women's cell I found my way to the nearest bunk bed. The bottom bed was empty, so I lay down. I used my leather jacket as a cover, dozing for a while. I woke shivering, wishing that all of that night's events were just a bad dream. My head hurt fiercely. One side of it felt ten times larger than the other side.

Daybreak came. Dawn filled the square cement room. Eight others snored away on several bunk beds lined against the wall. I sat on the dirty bare mattress. My bunk was in the middle of the room. A commode was at the opposite wall with a small basin. It had no doors, no cover, and no paper! Reluctantly I used it, then slowly washed my face. Then I dragged myself back onto the mattress. I wouldn't have moved if I didn't need to.

I dozed again, to be awakened by some women trying to clean my face. Blood ran down my cheekbone to my neck. They offered me wet wash towels. I wondered where they got them. Everyone else cleaned the cell. That had to be cleaned before breakfast was served. I couldn't move, so I figured the hell with breakfast. The women were pretty nice to offer the towels that were part of their cleaning stuff. When they finished, though, the wet cement floor still smelled of sour food. Of this group of women, the youngest was dressed fairly well and she was quite pretty compared to the other older women, any of whom could pass as my mother. They definitely had the routine memorized; the cell was squeaky clean. A husky lady with muscular arms approached me from their huddle. I remember thinking I wouldn't want to tangle with her. "You need to sit up for a little while," she said, and helped me. Then they called out to the jailers. After a fast inspection, the jailers served breakfast.

By that time I couldn't move. Slowly I grabbed my head and braced it between my hands in order to move my whole body. Luckily, the husky lady balanced my body as I rolled onto my side in great pain.

I thanked her, and as the youngest one covered me with my jacket, I wondered how such a young lady with a nice personality could be accustomed to this environment. Even the husky lady possessing the battle scars was friendly and helpful.

Breakfast was a box of cereal torn open to make a bowl, burnt toast, butter, jam, and coffee. I dozed again for half an hour or so. When I woke, my breakfast still waited. I welcomed the cold coffee. The rest of my breakfast was shared by the three bigger women. Two of them looked more masculine than feminine. I was somewhat afraid, but the pain I experienced was worse than the fear.

Drinking the coffee, I suddenly realized those women had actually saved my breakfast for me. My cell mates were still hungry, yet even the husky ladies waited until I offered my breakfast to them. This was courtesy and compassion I hadn't expected. If anyone wanted it, they could easily have taken my coat. I relaxed.

All the women were friendly. The youngest tried to talk to me. She saw that I was in too much pain, and she demanded I be taken to the hospital. At first she called the jailer by name. There was no answer. She then grabbed a tin coffee cup and ran it back and forth several times across the bars. "Where in the hell are you guys?" she yelled. The jailers didn't come. With no luck, the husky lady explained the day's procedure to me.

It was Sunday. I feared Justin and I would spend the whole day in jail until Monday. Half my mind was on pain, and the other half wondered about our children. Just as predicted, by eleven o'clock Justin, John, and I were each taken to enter our plea and post bail. When my turn came, I was taken into the sheriff's office, where I was questioned.

I explained what had happened. My story matched John's story. Then I was taken back to the cell, but John was released after posting fifty dollars bail. I had to post a one hundred dollar bail, but I had no money on me. I started to panic. John told Justin. It was a good thing he had some money. Justin came to my cell. "I need one hundred dollars," I said.

Justin dug in his pockets.

John asked again in Navajo how much my bail was. I told him, "One hundred dollars," in English. He asked in Navajo why my bail was higher than his. I said, "They booked me for resisting arrest and obstructing an officer." John turned to Justin and said in Navajo, "She must have a hard fist and a mean temper like Elsie." They both laughed. Elsie is John's mother. She gets real mad and is said to beat his stepfather when he drinks.

Justin's bail was set at five hundred dollars, and he had to appear before the judge on Monday.

After eleven hours in jail, I was free, breathing fresh air outside. Grandma was waiting for me with Mae.

Mae had called Grandma right after we were arrested. Grandma went to Thoreau and picked up the kids. They were all safe at her home over the hill from the jail. The three of us discussed how to get Justin out of jail. He was being held because a knife was considered a deadly weapon.

Grandma heard the whole story from Mae and then from me. She was more worried than I. Justin had given me more money than was necessary to post bail. He had just cashed his paycheck. I told her, "I will need to call his employer."

I forgot about going to the hospital. Grandma had to remind me, but I insisted on waiting. Grandma was angry. "Why in the world did you two go out with John?" she asked. "Justin knows John and Mae drink too much. You guys shouldn't have joined in." After a while, I reminded her how difficult it was to change Justin's mind once he was set on doing something. She agreed. We both knew, though, that we needed to get a medicine man to help us. "Do you have any money left?" she asked.

"I have some. How much do you think we'll need?" I asked.

Grandpa Juan was the best medicine man to use in our situation. I automatically pictured him in my mind, and felt peaceful. I was glad Grandma chose him.

Juan was about eighty years old, but his warm personality, friendly smile, and joking manner made him appear much younger. He always wore turquoise earrings on both his ears. The flat turquoise was about one inch long and three-fourths of an inch in diameter with string strung through a tiny hole at one end. He also wore a beautiful old-style necklace of turquoise nuggets. It accented his oval, tan face and brought out his dancing eyes with his rosy high cheekbones. The turquoise made his white hair shine, regardless of if he wore a western or traditional velveteen shirt. The only thing he didn't wear was a traditional hair knot. His hair barely touched the nape of his neck. He stood about five feet tall in his Navajo handmade moccasins, alongside his cane made of oak. He was very jolly. I've seen him tease even his cat with the tip of his cane, in a joking manner. He talked to animals as if they understood him. Grandma and I journeyed to his home at Washington Pass, seventy miles away.

Luckily he was at home. Grandma briefly described the previous events that occurred. Juan knew exactly what needed to be done. He shook his head and placed his soft wrinkled hand on my shoulder. "I will help," he said. "And don't worry." He then gathered his paraphernalia.

It was evening. The sun was going down. The area grew chilly as the mountains blocked the sun. We took Juan back to Grandma's house. He spent the night there.

The children kept asking for Justin. I tried to calm them as I continued all my household duties and Justin's as well.

The next morning over breakfast, Juan told us of a dream he had overnight. He said the dream told him I had been forewarned of the recent events and I did nothing to stop them. We hadn't mentioned to him that my face was struck, only that the gun was fired, but he knew. He advised me to seek medical attention. Grandma wanted to take me to the hospital. I refused, still concerned for Justin. Grandma understood and didn't push.

Juan's interpretation of his dream ended on a good note. He saw Justin out of jail soon and free of charges. Anxious to get things rolling in that direction, all of us went to an area directly above the jail. There we made offerings and prayers. Juan's prayers this time were unusual. He asked the Holy People to handle my injury in a way they thought was fair, according to the way my attacker lived. I also noticed that a couple of other prayers and songs were altered slightly. Each time he clearly left the outcome of the events in the hands of the Holy People.

Throughout the prayers, Grandma and I searched our minds as to when we might have been forewarned of all this. As we all returned home, a crow appeared and passed directly over the windshield, screaming loudly at us.

Grandma and I looked at each other. We remembered. I searched the sky for the crow, but it had vanished. Hardly able to contain this information, Grandma spilled it out the minute we stepped in the house.

Juan had no information from us about the crow's message to me, nor of the injury I sustained, until we told him. Yet this was revealed to him the night before, in his dream. The crow appeared to me weeks before the incident. In a way, that warning was still with me all those times I couldn't pass a mirror without looking at my face. In a sense, I was expecting injury to it, without realizing it. Now, to correct the disharmony, I needed to make offerings and prayers. This was planned for a later time.

It was enough to know just this information Juan provided. Justin still waited in jail for our help.

Grandma and I arrived at the jail about ten o'clock on Monday. Arraignments were to begin then. Justin stood before the judge at about eleven-thirty to enter his pleas of "not guilty." Bail was set at five hundred dollars, but could not be posted until after one o'clock. At two-thirty Justin was released. Relieved and exhausted, we went home to cook lunch. Juan smiled when he saw Justin.

The children were excited. Everyone rushed around as if nothing had happened. I busied myself slicing potatoes while the meat cooked. Just as Justin brought in wood, I looked up to smile at him. Then the room started to spin. I heard a crash and everything turned black again.

The next thing I realized Justin was carrying me to the couch. Next, we were on our way to the hospital. I could hear people talking, but their voices sounded like they were coming from a tunnel.

We waited in the emergency room before I was sent to X-ray. The technician asked, "What hit your face?" He wanted to know when it happened. When I told him, he said, "You mean you walked around for two days like that? Does it hurt?" He then took me to the farthest wall where my X-rays hung, and he pointed out a crack in my right cheekbone. My face was swollen pretty bad then. He said, "After the swelling goes down, the right side of your face will severely sink inward."

I was stunned and shocked. I asked, "How sure are you?" I asked to see the X-ray a second time. That time I paid attention. I still wasn't sure, so I settled on his expert opinion. I mumbled thanks and returned to the emergency room with the X-rays. The doctor returned, took a quick look and prescribed a couple of morphine pills to ease the pain.

"That's all? Are you serious?" I asked. I then relayed the technician's point of view. He immediately called for an ENT (ears, nose and throat) doctor to come view the X-rays.

Justin brought in the lab technician. The technician pointed to the crack, a fine hairline crack. I myself couldn't really make it out. All conferred among themselves, then informed me of my choices: walk around the rest of my life with one side of my face sunk in, or have surgery.

I chose surgery. The minute I lay down in the hospital bed, I was out. I slept through the evening. I woke around midnight, my head throbbing again. The nurse entered with a needle full of medicine to ease the pain. The nurse told me that Justin had stayed with me until security chased him away.

Surgery was set at six the next morning. I didn't have any feelings about it. I wasn't scared, just so full of pain. Justin arrived just as I was being wheeled out of the elevator near the operating room.

The only part of surgery I remember is that the operating room was cold. I shivered at first from the cold, then from the pain below my right eye. I must have moved my head hard to the side. The doctor had already started to cut beneath it and that area wasn't numb. I heard his angry voice, then I was out again.

I woke to find Justin at my bedside about three that afternoon. The pain was severe. My whole head felt ten times as large, with hammers pounding inside. Ten stitches were taken underneath my right eye. Inside my mouth were six stitches. The surgeons cut below my eyelid and inside my mouth to get to the area of my cheekbone. My cheekbone was wired together and put back in place.

Afterwards, I couldn't feel the right side of my face for a long time, especially when I had a runny nose. I felt a throbbing pain when the weather was cold or cloudy. Every time the weather changed, and my face hurt, I thought of that man with the shotgun. After surgery I had prayers and offerings done.

Justin's trial was approaching, so we employed a good lawyer. The bar owner who cracked my cheekbone had never been arrested. Justin's lawyer, a highly respected upstanding citizen, persuaded me not to press charges until after the trial. Justin and I believed in him so we followed his advice. All along, though, he was helping the prosecutor.

After a week of testimony, charges against Justin were dropped for lack of evidence. There were no eyewitnesses. The real story was revealed. The boy who was stabbed had been attacked by his friend in an argument. Those two boys were under the age of twenty-one, yet they were regular customers at that bar.

A week later Justin and I decided to press charges against the bar owner. On our way to town we were stopped by Justin's boss. He said, "The bar owner's wife shot herself in the head. She did it right in front of her husband last night." A cold chill ran down my spine. Justin and I looked at each other. The next thing we heard was that the bar owner had gone crazy.

Bueno-Bye

A. A. Hedge Coke

Dusk
Mountain View transforms to street scene
babies crying
children throwing up
hitting cars with sticks
men cursing
men drinking up, playing
guitars
Women walking alone
silent, hiding
smell of salsa lingers
on night air
Vehicles cruising through parking lot
chemicals for sale
lonely hearts seeking comfort
in strangers
Footsteps on metal stairs
reinforced in concrete
vaguely resembling adobe
Because
        this is
                Santa Fe

▼ ▼ ▼ ▼ ▼ ▼

Carnival Lights

Stacey Velarde

The sun was like a big piece of candy sitting on the horizon. It was just like when she was little and her cousin-sister used to ride that big ol' bay and buckskin all afternoon while her dad and uncles roped. Those were the days when a hot dusty rodeo was the family event of the summer. Kellie's family was important to her when she was that little, and so were all the things they believed in and all the rodeos they went to together.

Things were so crazy now. She sat at a run-down little gas station somewhere out on the Navajo reservation, at a place called Tohatchi. The young cowboy she just met a few weeks earlier stood out by the road waiting to flag down the next vehicle. She decided to try again to loosen the chewed-up lug nuts on the trailer. The tire was so far gone, it looked like shredded black paper. The horses stood in their head-to-tail formation swatting flies under the scrawny little tree, waiting patiently. Everything out here seemed so slow, and nobody but her was in a hurry. She was the only one who ever got irritated. Everyone else—even animals—was so excruciatingly patient!

Navajoland was so desolate and dusty and deserted—or at least to strangers it was. This was not her home, but it felt so exciting, or inviting or—something. She couldn't quite tell you exactly what it was she craved out here. When she wasn't here, she just knew she was missing out on something. The weather in the summer fueled her excitement. On the weekends, during the small tribal fairs and at the rodeos, the sun baked and burned everything and everybody, and the wind whipped and flapped anything that wasn't tied down. During the week, you could see the dark gray clouds building up to the wet roaring rain the Navajos called the male rain. It was like the storms knew there was something tense and trembling back behind her stomach, back where excitement and passion are born. When these storms cleared everything left behind was wet and cold and muddy-smelling. The storms imitated the mystery of the land and the way of life and the people out here. There was something brewing behind the clouds and the wind, and one of these days she would find out what was there.

The weekends were the best. That's when everybody congregated at the run-down little barbed wire arenas for the weekend, ready for competition and camaraderie. They all craved the same fix. The dust and the wind and the sun and everything mingled and the smell was wonderful. It smelled like fast horses and trucks and trailers and steers and calves and winning lots of cash and, well, rodeo. The contestants were here for the glory and because they had all been born into it. This was their way of life. The young cowboys pranced around for the lovesick, awestruck girls who drove from all over the reservation. Cowboys called them Buckle Bunnies, and they came to watch and cheer, just hoping they would be the next in line for the attentions of these boys. The lure of money and local fame attracted all the young single cowboys and cowgirls, and of course, all the well-known rodeo families. It was the only thing she ever knew and wanted, but now it was starting to be out of control and different.

An old green Chevy pickup rolled slowly down the highway and finally stopped in front of the gas station. A short old man with white stubble poking out from under a greasy baseball cap got out and hobbled to a nearby faucet. She stood up and stared at the young cowboy she was with, hoping he was thinking what she was thinking. He didn't move. . . . He didn't even turn around. . . . Why was he being so stupid? She barked at him with obvious irritation in her voice, "Andrew! Come here!" He looked up and stumbled back to the trailer.

"Why don't you go talk to him and ask him if he has a lug wrench? We probably won't make it to Window Rock on time, but we still need to change the tire before we go anywhere—right?"

"Who is he?" he asked, smiling the way she remembered Gomer Pyle used to smile on TV. She realized she wasn't traveling with the brightest calf roper on the reservation.

"Does it matter? Just be friendly! I would ask, except he probably doesn't speak English, and since you're the only one of us who speaks Navajo, you'll have to do it, man. Sheesh!"

He chuckled and stumbled toward the old man. He sure does stumble a lot for a calf roper, she thought. He stood at a distance from the truck, looking in at the old man. Andrew didn't say anything—apparently he knew the old man would respond in time. As they spoke she could see Andrew motioning in the air in the shape of a tire iron, then pointing at the trailer. The old man nodded and got his tire iron from the back of his pickup and handed it to the cowboy. Andrew trotted back to the trailer and went to work on the stripped lug nuts.

The old man hobbled over and stood by watching. "*Yá'át'ééh,*" he said, smiling and nodding at her.

She smiled and nodded back, "Hi . . . " She hoped that answering in English would indicate she didn't speak Navajo. Finally Andrew stood up and heaved the spare in the back of the truck.

He returned the tire iron to the old man and thanked him, rather shyly, *"Ah'ehe."*

They loaded the horses and jumped back in the pickup. She got behind the wheel, and she pulled out onto the highway toward Window Rock with her foot mashed to the floor. "You think we can still make it? It's only six o'clock . . . "

Andrew didn't say much. "Well, let's stop at the Giant station first. We can stay with my friend Curtis if we're too late."

She knew full well what that meant. He intended to stop at the Giant and waste enough time to be too late to make it all the way into Window Rock, then go to Curt's house and put the horses up and go to the bar later. The past two weeks with Andrew had been the same—go to the rodeos (and usually they both won some money), rush home and put the horses up, shower and go out on the town. The girls were always waiting for Andrew to arrive, and inevitably there would be a scene. She was glad to be with him, and he was obviously proud to be seen with her, but she realized he just couldn't resist the attention from the young girls. She also knew that out here on the reservation, the young girls just couldn't resist the lure of the night life and possibility of catching one of these young cowboy heroes.

They pulled into the station, and for the first time all day, she felt hungry and dusty and tired. It was now close to seven o'clock p.m.—the rodeo started thirty minutes ago, and the entries closed over an hour ago. The cool air and the purple rays on the horizon toward Zuni made her suddenly fatigued. Tonight would be a good night for staying home, maybe soaking in the tub for a while, and falling asleep in front of the TV—just the two of them. She knew he'd never agree. This was Saturday night, the last night for Andrew to go out this weekend, and he just couldn't disappoint his fans. She had learned how to look at the floor and shrink behind Andrew when drunk women followed him around at the bars and rodeos. If she looked them in the eye while standing beside Andrew, they would try to scratch her eyes out. They never needed a reason—just looking at them was reason enough. Andrew always just stood there, enjoying the attention. He was no help at all. Another scene, another fight, another drunken argument was all it meant to her.

Her daddy pulled into a gas station a few miles from the rodeo arena to fill the gas tanks and stock up on ice and pop and chips and all the regular rodeo food. It was mid-morning and the small reservation town was packed with out-of-town relatives and tourists, and it was already humming. All around, the air smelled like a summer fair or holiday. There was a carnival by the rodeo arena, and a powwow in the high school gym. Later tonight there would be a western dance and of course the carnival would last until the wee hours of the morning.

There were bright posters in the window of the gas station that read:

Come to the annual Tribal Fair and Rodeo!
Lots of family fun and entertainment including:
All-Indian Rodeo
Stock Contractor: Rockin' Bar J & Co. from Socorro, NM
Announcer: Harrison Yazzie from Chinle, AZ
• Powwow
• Pony Express Races
• Motor-Cross races
• All-Indian Basketball Tournaments
• Western Dance with the Navajo Sundowners
performing live at the Community Center Gym.
Last Weekend in July, 1972
Dulce, NM

The little girl crawled out from under the blanket in the bed of the pickup with hopelessly tangled hair and hay crumbs in her clothes. She gathered her small herd of toy horses and sat on the side of the pickup watching her daddy fill up the tank. The sun was already beating down on her dark hair, and she knew she was going to die if they didn't hurry up and get to the rodeo. She could see the carnival and the dust from people warming up their horses in the arena. Tonight, the lights of the carnival would light up the sky, but for now, the rodeo and her cousins waited, and she could already feel a good hot dusty rodeo day coming on.

They drove by the carnival and she saw that some of their cousins were already there. As soon as they parked, she was jumping up and down, begging to go join her cousins at the carnival.

Her mom just gave her a pat on the head. "We just got here! Daddy hasn't even unloaded the horses yet. You have to wait."

She could wait—for now. Her daddy began to throw a saddle on her old bay gelding, and her attention was quickly drawn away from the carnival. Her mommy put on her little brown-tipped boots, then her daddy set her onto the big bay, and she trotted off to the arena where some of her other cousins were. The carnival wasn't very exciting to her yet. Not without the lights anyway. They wouldn't be turned on till the sun went down, and that was along time from now.

He broke her silence for her. "I just talked to Curtis. He said to come over and eat. He wants to know if we wanna go to the bar tonight . . . "

She rubbed her eyes and said, "I suppose. I don't have very much money, though."

He tried to act innocent, as though he had no ulterior motives. "I'll pay for you. I always pay for my girl."

These reservation guys, they think they're so smooth, she thought. "Okay. We have to put up the horses first. Can we leave them at Curt's house?"

Her enthusiasm was melting fast. She was just about to see what was there behind the lights at night, and the music. Only now it was getting scary. The dark gray clouds and the carnival lights off in the distance were just hiding the dark scary places where the red-eyed men and women stood. Where men told nasty jokes in Navajo, and women threatened you. Where the little kids waited, crying and hiding on the floor of the pickup for their mommy and daddy to come out and take them home. Where the sweet smell of wine and the bitter smell of beer and despair made your eyes water, and where the red and blue lights fooled you into believing this was all so glamorous and exciting—not dark and scary. As they pulled into Curt's driveway, she saw Curt and some woman standing out by the corrals, both clutching a silver can to their chest.

The little girl trotted around the rodeo grounds all day on her big bay gelding with her cousin-sister. They climbed on and off and played together—completely oblivious to the scorching heat and powdery dust hanging in the air. They played under the bleachers with toy horses and dirty plastic spoons and pebbles and dirt and all the other treasures they could only find under the bleachers at a rodeo. Her shirt was all covered with orange pop and dirt. She had to keep reminding her mommy that she wanted to go to the carnival, just like the big kids. Each time she got the same frustrating response: "You're too little to go by yourself. Wait till after the rodeo, and Daddy and I will take you for an hour or so before we go over to Grandma's to eat." There was something they were hiding from her. Something about the carnival and why only big kids could go there, especially after dark. She had heard stories about it. Her older cousin-sister said that you can't go there unless you're old enough. It was still a bit too early in the day and she was still having a bit too much fun to worry about what she was missing out on at the carnival.

Eventually, the rodeo was over. Her mommy and daddy stood by the pickup sharing a beer with her auntie and uncle. People began to load up and go to their hotels or house or wherever they were staying this weekend. The music from the carnival was getting louder now. Her cousin-sister had already left with some other big kids for the carnival without her. As the air cooled and the dust and excitement of the rodeo settled, the little girl began to tug on her daddy's belt loop harder and harder because her mommy and daddy kept forgetting the time. She thought she might be forced to cry if they continued to ignore her like this. If they didn't hurry, there wouldn't be enough time to take her to the carnival tonight before they left for the dance. They promised her that this year she was finally big enough and they would take her to the carnival.

Then, she saw the lights come on. The Ferris wheel looked like a big bright-red piece of a candy in the dark purple sky. Music could be heard all over town now. She was being left out, just because her mommy and daddy were so slow! How long were they going to make her suffer like this?

Curtis and his woman climbed on the fence next to Kellie and Andrew. They watched the last purple dusty rays turn into night. The woman reminded Kellie of the ones who roam the streets of Gallup at night under the neon. Even the red and blue light in the bars and under the street signs didn't help hide their drunken ugliness. Just like these women, she wore a tight, frayed T-shirt that unfortunately left nothing to the imagination, and filthy jeans and boots that had probably been slept in for a week. She wondered where Curt had found her and why she was even here. Curt always struck her as one of those not-so-good looking cowboys who could have most any woman on the reservation just because he was one of the local Navajo heroes who had qualified to rope once at the INFR in Albuquerque. Even though the next house was several miles down the dirt road, she thought she smelled steaks cooking from somewhere. Curt's place was behind the hill at Black Hat and they could see the lights of Gallup from there getting brighter and brighter as it got darker outside.

Finally, they climbed off the fence and walked to the trailer house. Curt and Andrew were starting to talk louder now, and Andrew had his arm and most of his weight around her neck. She could feel the muscles in his back when she put her hand there, and she could smell his oily, sweaty hair underneath his straw hat. Curt's trailer was filthy. The smell of cigarette smoke and beer and rotten food slowly oozed into her nose and made her stomach feel warm and greasy. She held her breath so she wouldn't retch all over his moldy-looking couch.

She wasn't sure why or how she had gotten here and it was all getting out of control and scary. It seemed wonderful at first that this handsome young cowboy was taking her to all these rodeos and showing her the carnival lights. Those lights were getting so dim, yet they showed things a little more clearly. She was sad and almost sick. All she wanted to do was lay down in front of her great-grandma's pot-bellied stove and smell the burning piñon inside like all those times she waited for her mom and dad to come home from the rodeo dances. But here she was, with people she didn't know, out on the Navajo reservation, and all the fun and excitement that she imagined was there when she was little was nowhere to be found.

She stood in the small slimy bathroom crying over the sink. She turned on the cold water and tried to wash away the muddy tears and cool off her sunburned face. She stood up and looked at herself in the mirror and tried to deny that she knew she needed to go home now. Andrew had nothing in common with her besides rodeo—he had nothing to offer her. This way of life had nothing to offer her, even though it was the only way of life she had ever known. Andrew knocked on the door, then walked in. He set her suit bag on the floor and grabbed her from behind. She smelled the beer on his breath, and he began swaying and leaning on her. He smiled at her in the mirror and as he spoke, she was barely able to stomach his breath and his drunkenness. "Just put some different jeans on and let's go—you look fine. All the ladies will jus' be jealous if you get too good lookin". His thick, choppy Navajo accent was getting thicker and uncontrollable as he drank. "We'll jus' go drinkin' an' dancin 'gain. Da bar's gon' be packed. I jus' wann' go have fun. Let's go, den."

Once more they drove toward the carnival lights in town. She could already see the blue and red neon flashing in downtown Gallup from the top of the hill. In a few hours, people would be drinking, dancing, dying, and fading under the lights. Mothers would leave their babies with a relative if they could, or in their drunken stupor they might just abandon them back home. They were all drawn to the lights, like moths. They couldn't control it anymore. The rodeo heroes tried to justify their pathetic drunken lives, but she was beginning to realize that they were the same as the dying alcoholics. They dressed differently and they were maybe a little well-known, but they were the same. Alcoholism was for "drunk Indi'ns"—not them. They were just here for a good time after the rodeo. They had a home to go to, so therefore they were better than the "Tradin' Pos' Cowboys" who spent their nights and their youths under the lights in Gallup.

They pulled into the parking lot in front of the hotel bar where the line to get in was already out the door. Behind the building she saw the sad, scraggly men and women begging for change, and she even saw a small boy clinging to the leg of a woman who was being pushed off balance by another pitiful, oily drunk. Tonight it would be as easy to walk past these creatures and pretend she didn't see. The lights were showing things all too clearly, just like a bright fluorescent beam focusing on the disease in front of her.

Andrew walked in the bar with his arm around Kellie and his black felt hat tipped to one side. He stopped at the edge of the dance floor, threw his chest out and stood there for a moment looking like a rooster in a hen house. A young boy tapped him on the shoulder smiling, and swaying to and fro slightly. Andrew looked at him but said nothing. Kellie guessed from his plaid western shirt and his uncreased black hat that he probably didn't get away from the reservation much.

He gathered up some confidence and tapped Andrew on the shoulder again. "Aren't you Andrew Nez? I seen you rope a calf in Albuquerque at the INFR this year. . . . Can I buy you a drink?"

"I already got one."

She wanted to shake the young man's hand, or something, but before she could do anything Andrew pulled on her arm and they walked away. She looked over her shoulder to smile at him and shrugged her shoulders. The young man stood there looking foolish with that same drunken smile, only now looking at the floor.

The little girl stood on a wooden bench behind her great-grandma's small black house while her mommy swabbed off all the dust and stickiness of the day. The wash rag felt cool against her tummy and back and neck. She desperately fought the sleepiness creeping up on her. They had just finished eating steaks cooked over a fire out back. From their location on the hill, she could see the lights at the carnival beginning to glow as the sky turned purple. The sun was fading, and the cool air seemed to come alive with western music and lights. Her mommy and daddy were dressed in starched black jeans and shiny boots. They seemed to tap their toes to music the little girl couldn't hear. They smiled to each other and laughed, and they ignored her sobs and tears. Why couldn't she go? If the dance they were going to was so wonderful and so much fun, why wouldn't they take her, too? What did they do at "the dance"? What did it look like? Was it dark inside? Maybe it was like the carnival. . . . She just couldn't bear the thought of having to be left out of such excitement. Her mommy pulled her jammies over her head and fastened them to the bottoms, then picked her up and carried her into the small house that had no running water or electricity. She put her into the small bed beside her grandma and wiped her tears, then her daddy came in and bent over to kiss her on the forehead. The wool blankets were rough and smelled like piñon smoke and Vicks. She listened to the pickup outside the window as it bounced away down the dirt road. Just before she fell asleep, she watched her grandma sitting beside the pot-bellied stove singing an old Apache lullaby, feeling tired and loved and maybe a little left out and frustrated. The only other sound was way off in the distance at the carnival, and there was a faint light coming through the window from the bright red and white flashing carnival lights.

Inside the bar, the smoke and the haze and the music all jumbled inside her head, and she thought she heard the words to a song her daddy used to sing:

Don't tell them that you're crying,
just say, "Smokey the Bar"

Thirty minutes ago she saw Andrew in the corner of the dance floor with some girls. They were trying to pick him up off the floor, but they were drunk, so they only managed to step on his hat. She stood with her back leaning on the bar watching people laugh and drink and cry and fight and drown and choke. Their old way of life was being replaced by this dismal existence. She glanced around and saw the young man who had offered Andrew a drink staggering toward the door. The smell filled her nose and eyes and she couldn't breathe or see. The room spun and all she could see was a tunnel in front of her. As she moved toward the door, her feet seemed to hit the floor harder each time. Finally, as she stepped outside, the cold air rushed over her like water and she moved around to the edge of the parking lot and threw up until she was out of breath and her eyes watered. She stood there bent over for a minute, staring at the puddle at her feet, thinking about home.

She stood up and she saw the mesa toward Zuni. She filled her nose and lungs with the cold air and walked to her pickup. Her head was filled with an old Apache lullaby as she turned the road to Curt's house. She figured that if she drove all night, she would get to her parent's place on the Apache reservation just at dawn. They could eat breakfast together like they used to, and her dad would probably want to go practice a little roping, and then maybe haul some trash to their dump. All she saw now were the stars and the mesa tops, and all she heard were the old songs her grandma used to sing to her. The carnival lights were behind here, and now it was time to go home. A good time for going home . . .

▼ ▼ ▼ ▼ ▼ ▼

Storm

Brent Toadlena

the psychos and weirdos paced
the length of the Greyhound linoleum
but you never came
so I wept for those old nights
by Grandma's fire
and the scent of birthing ewes

soon this city will become me
as I struggle and revolt its
wretched grasp of sin
and unlimited supply of poison—

towards dawn the rain will cease
and take with it my loneliness
and heartache for the sandstone
and sage of my home—

they've always had that power over me

Why There Are Blackberries Around Cedar Trees
(Adapted from a Squamish Legend As Told by Charles A. Sneatlum, Sr.)

Karen and Wally Strong

Narrator Long ago when all things were human, the teachings of the elders of the tribe were the "golden rule." If you disobeyed this rule, your life would be cut short, and you would die young. This would shame and embarrass your family, and they would have to help you right your wrongdoing. *(Scene opens. A young man is coming home from hunting, tired and hungry.)*

Young Man Whew! Am I ever tired! I must have packed this ten miles to get home! *(He puts down an animal in front of his wife.)* Bring me something to eat!

Wife You'll just have to wait! Everyone has eaten and there is nothing left. I'll cook this! *(She takes the animal, skins it, and starts to cook it over a fire.)*

Young Man This meat isn't cooked enough! I can't eat it!

Wife Oh! Give it to me. . . . You are always complaining. A person just can't try hard enough for you!

Great Changer Tsk! Listen to her! She can't even be polite to her husband! Such a person should be far away from other people! What can I do?

Narrator The Great Changer goes up to the young wife and talks to her.

Wife Who are you? What are you doing in our home? You weren't invited!

Great Changer I thought that I could help you . . .

Wife Help me! Help me do what?

Great Changer Well, let me finish my sentence! I wanted to help you so that you could cook better . . .

Wife Help me cook better! I was in a hurry and put the food too far from the fire. I know that. Now what else do *you* think you can help me do?

Great Changer You are very rude. You won't even let me finish what I am saying.

Wife *(Shouting)* Who do you think you are? I don't know you. I'm not going to listen to you.

Great Changer *(Quietly)* I am Doo-qwee-bulthl.

Wife Who?

Great Changer I am Doo-qwee-bulthl, the Great Changer.

Wife Oh, no! What have I done!

Great Changer You can't even be polite to strangers! I am going to punish you! I am going to put you on top of a cedar tree where *you* will not have to be polite to anyone!

Narrator The Great Changer lifts the young wife up into the air and carries her to the top of the cedar tree.

Wife Help! Help! Put me down! I'll be good, I promise!

Narrator It's already too late for the young wife to make amends. Maybe someone in the forest can help her now.

Wife Help! Help! Help me, please!

Deer Who is it? What are you doing up there?

Wife It's me! Oh, Skay-qwats, help me get down!

Deer Oh, it's you! How did you get up there?

Wife Doo-qwee-bulthl, the Great Changer, has put me up here to punish me!

Deer Well, then, you must have deserved it.

Wife Skay-qwats! Help me.

Deer I don't know if I can, but I'll go get someone to help you!

Narrator Skay-qwats, the deer, runs to the creek where the animals are getting a drink, shouting his message.

Deer Doo-qwee-bulthl, the Great Changer, has punished the young wife! He has put her on top of a cedar tree! Who can help her get down? *(Animals gather around the deer.)*

Raven Anyone, I repeat, *anyone* can easily rescue this lady. Just let me have a chance. I, the Raven, will show you how it can be done easily. *(With thumbs in his lapels, the Raven swaggers around with his wings to his chest. Everyone begins laughing.)*

Raccoon *(Giggling)* Go ahead, Raven. Let us see you rescue the young lady.

Narrator *(The Raven begins by ruffling and smoothing his feathers.)* Once every feather on the Raven is in place, he begins his task, a fine figure of a bird.

Raven Out of the way! Out of the way! I need plenty of room. *(Looks up.)* Young wife! Are you ready to be saved?

Wife Oh, yes! Please hurry!

Narrator	The Raven, step by step, climbs the bottom part of the tree. . . . Uh, oh! There he goes! *(The Raven slides back down the tree.)*
Bear	What happened, Raven?
Raven	Oh, I wasn't putting my claws into the bark! This time I will.
Narrator	The Raven approaches the cedar tree, gallantly swinging his arms. This time he is serious! *(The Raven swings his arms widely back and forth. He reaches the bottom of the tree, shakes his tail feathers, and begins his climb.)*
Beaver	Look! He is climbing higher this time!
Raccoon	He won't make it! He's slowing down, he's getting tired!
Raven	Whew! I'll just rest here a minute. . . . Whaaaaaaaaaaa! *(He falls; everyone laughs.)*
Narrator	The Raven has failed again. This time he has fallen and is knocked out cold.
Bear	What a silly bird that Raven is. I can climb trees, and I am stronger than him. I will rescue the lady. *(The Bear begins his climb, moving slowly.)*
Beaver	The bear is too big! He is bending the branches on the tree!
Cougar	Watch out, Es-chut-qwad, the tree is breaking! Come back down!
Bear	*(Comes down.)* If I was smaller, I might have saved her.
Wife	Can't any of you help me? I'll be good! I don't want to stay up here! *(Begins to cry.)*
Cougar	Please stop crying! We're going to send someone else to help you!
Beaver	Okay! Who's next? How about you, Cougar?

Cougar	I'm too big. . . . Let's send the Squirrel.
Squirrel	I'll go, but I want the Raccoon to go get the other birds to help me get her down. *(The Raccoon goes to find the other birds, and the Squirrel goes part of the way up and comes down. The Raven flaps his wings.)*
Bear	The Raven is waking up!
Raven	*(Yawns and stretches.)* That was a nice rest. Now I am ready to finish what I started! *(Everyone rolls around laughing. The Raven gets up, flexes his muscles, gives a victory war whoop and runs to the cedar tree.)*
Narrator	Here he goes for his third attempt to save the lady. *(He runs up three-fourths of the way, and he slips and slips and slips all the way down the tree.)*
Raven	Shucks! It's just not my day today! Somebody else will just have to do it! *(Leaves the stage.)*
Raccoon	*(Returning with the birds.)* We're back! Now to find a way to get the lady down! Owl . . . ?
Owl	I don't know what you want me to do. I'm not sure of daytime procedures. Bluejay, what do you think?
Bluejay	I fly from branch to branch. I don't think people can do that, can they? Oh, I know—Red-Headed Woodpecker can make steps for her to climb down by pecking holes in the tree trunk!
All Animals	Yes! That's a good idea! *(Woodpecker goes up and starts to work.)*
Woodpecker	*(Coughing and gasping.)* Ow! This tree causes splinters to get in my throat! *(Comes back down.)*
Owl	Where is that little bird I've seen climb up the trees? Whoo is he?

Squirrel	Is this who you mean? *(Points to a little bird.)*
Little Bird	Who, me? Well . . . I can show her what to do, but she will have to be very careful. *(Goes up.)*
Narrator	The Little Bird is leading the young Wife from side to side down the tree.
Wife	Ow! Ow! The tree branches are scratching and bruising me! I will surely bleed to death before I get to the bottom!
Narrator	They have reached the bottom. The Wife is bruised and bleeding from the scratches and cuts she got climbing down.
Owl	We all helped rescue you. Now it is up to you to make sure that you do not bring the wrath of Doo-qweee-bulthl, the Great Changer, on yourself.
Wife	Oh! I'll be good. I promise!
Narrator	She leaves to find her own way. *(Thunder sounds, the trees shake, and the leaves fall. The Great Changer enters.)*
Great Changer	The young wife has learned her lesson. Who helped her down from the cedar tree?
All Animals	We did!
Great Changer	Why did you take the law into your own hands when it was not up to you to decide?
Little Bird	I was the one who showed her the way down the tree.
Great Changer	From now on you will have no name. All of you animals will see this little bird going from side to side on tree trunks. He will be a reminder to you of what can happen to you when you try to be something other than what you have been created for.

Narrator The Great Changer came to the encampment and told the people what happened to the bird and, as a reminder to the people of what can happen when you try to be something other than what you have been created for, the Great Changer made the blood of the Wife permanent on this land by turning it into blackberries, which are usually found around the bottoms of huge cedar trees to this day.

Special Note to the Stage Person
The cedar tree should be an A-frame ladder with paper attached for the trunk and branches. That way animals can climb up and down.

▼ ▼ ▼ ▼ ▼ ▼

Into the Hand of the Great Healer

Floyd Yazzie

Mr. Becenti lies in a wet, stained bed all day.
The murmurs and urine tell me he is always there.
He lies there, motionless, from early morning
To sundown . . . but he is not dead.
"My Little Brother, my long journey here is almost over, and yours stretches out before you," he tells me. "I wait here for the Great Healer."
An old TV and an even older white nurse
Are the only threads between us.
The chasm of generations, time, and language
Can easily be overlooked.
My dessert and coffee are always his.
"My Little Brother, where are you going?" he says when he awakes. "I wait for the Great Healer."
On Sundays, his overly polite family
Exits and enters.
They arrive with freshly-cut flowers, rosaries,
Cards that say, "Get Well Grandpa."
They pray until tears came to their eyes.
"My Little Brother, my journey is almost over," he says as they cart me away.
Three days after they cut me open, I stare cold
Into the fuzzy screen.
His story of how he will triumphantly sail
Through the window and into the hands of the Great Healer
Echoes in my drugged head.
All their prayers, rosaries, and tears did not stop it.
The days pass like a blurred stream of codeine,
Applesauce, and more codeine.
I hear no murmurs, smell no urine, and eat no
Applesauce.

Oh, Saint Michael

Carlson Vicenti

Oh, Saint Michael,
I can't find a car.
Not Akar, the bearded white man with the nappy head wrapped in a blue bath towel. The wanna be "sick" that forgot his true culture after an overdose of acid at a Dead show in Philly, PA. Who wound up kissing the ass cheeks of the great plastic idol, Iky Poo Poo, stolen from the Hari Krishnas. That horrible day when all the monks across California, by disaster or miracle, spilled Clorox bleach in their laundry—orange frocks and nasty habits—and all turned white and they took it as a holy sign. So they put rings in their noses and wore tight black leather, moved to San Fran, and walked hand in hand on the Wharf, ripping farts that couldn't be heard because of heavy traffic behind.

Oh, no, Saint Michael.
I'm looking for the smog cars, the ones that give me the pleasure of waiting fifteen minutes to walk forty paces. The kind I fear will bust my head open by a stroke of good luck and bad timing. The one like Delores drives. You know her? The coke-snorting pseudo-intellectual psychic healer. The one I met in a bar. She saw my aura, and I asked her if that was some kind of yoga bull. She sensed my inner anger, so I told her to go to hell, or give me some of that white hippy sexual healing she offers Skins, because she lost her identity to Wonderbread and Cheerios, or was it that accident on Cerrillos? She said having sex with Skins would take her back four lives ago when she was a great medicine man in the lower Bronx, where she was born behind Mario's pizzeria to Maria, the overworked Italian girl making a delivery.

Oh, no, Saint Michael.
I'm looking for the fast cars that have four crushing wheels and a demonic engine, and screwed up dead drivers from all over the world, and mental states, seeking fake karma in the barren facade of Santa Fe.
Do you know what I mean?

Go on now, Saint Michael, drive

▼ ▼ ▼ ▼ ▼ ▼

Spirit in Me

Esther G. Belin

When I was young I met the spirit & I knew I didn't want it, but the choice was never mine. This is for all my relations.

i go back to the day i was driving
in the pit of the painted desert near lower greasewood on the navajo
reservation
that day i was driving my mom's truck
not feeling anything
except the spirit
the spirit of alcohol chased me &
rode beside & held my hand & led me to
thinking of a few days before
the day of the 6.3 earthquake in the california desert
when my mom's voice shook the house
as she told me
the spirit of alcohol caught nathan &
he isn't coming back
imprisoned by his own body destroying itself
& all i could think about is how i love him & how we loved each
other & back then years ago it was real & it was good & the
memory made me cry cuz i never wanted him dead
only healed
weaned from alcohol
& now he's dying & the parts of me i gave him are dying too & i
cry harder cuz the parts of himself he gave me
the talents he never used that i use now to stay alive won't die when
he does
& i start to drive faster cuz the spirit of alcohol is still walking
alongside me
& i hear it talking sweet &
singing old songs &
i almost want to sing along like i know the words &

i just have to remember &
i think about his spirit
cuz i see it in me
so back when i used to drink
i never could drink miller lite
cuz that meant the spirit got you
caged
like nathan & daddy & uncle john & aunt rosita
& me too maybe
cuz i see them in me & i'm caged like them
but in a different way
cuz i can see them when they can't & i can see the spirit scream out of them in rage &
i can love them & they can't love back
cuz the spirit took it outta them &
all i know how to do is keep loving them
believing i'm like the reservation deep & wide
nestling spirits greater than alcohol.

▼ ▼ ▼ ▼ ▼ ▼

THE HYATT, THE MAORI, AND THE YANOAMA

Irvin Morris

After supper I cut a slice of watermelon and sat on the porch steps, spitting seeds and watching the shadow of the mountains behind my home stretch across the valley. As they touched the horizon, there was a final smolder of color. The pale cliffs of Chaco Canyon gleamed like inlays of mica on the edge of the world. Gray thunderheads tinged with orange and pink glowed over Torréon and the Sierra Nacimiento. They were Holy People come from the south, dressed in icy robes of water. They had come in answer to our prayers once again, bringing nothing less than life itself.

Anaasázi. I imagined the canyon sacred with the jingle of copper bells, vibrant with voices, bright with parrot feathers. The Ancient Ones dancing. Prayer in motion. The plaza at Pueblo Bonito awash with firelight and the thunder of drums rolling like waves through the canyon. Far to the east, a rainbow glowed in the last light.

Ahaláane, I thought. How better to express the joy and awe?

I sank into the deep cushions of the sofa, and the indigo landscape outside dropped below the cluttered sill. A gilded dragon. Brass elephants. A pair of rosy-cheeked youth, a boy and girl caught in mid-stride, a wooden bucket held between them. They had been on their way back from the well when the ceramist froze them for all time. I aimed the remote and the television came alive, hissing.

Thunderous applause. Hysterical laughter. Then tight faces as Eddie Murphy began talking about black and white. The dog barked. I punched the mute button and the gate hinges squeaked twice. There was a knock on the door. I flicked on the porch light and Frank, my neighbor and in-law, squinted in the sudden glare. He stepped quickly into the room, trailing a faint wake of rain-scented air. His expression was grim.

"Don't tell me," I said. "Is she . . . "

"She is," he nodded. "Again."

While I rummaged for flashlights in the kitchen drawers, he told me that he had just got back from pulling a cow out of the mud at the watering hole. "That took all afternoon, and then I come home to this mess," he said, shaking his head. "Dammit." He'd left the oldest girl in charge, but she'd been too busy gabbing on the phone to notice anything.

The last time the old lady had disappeared, they found her huddled in a clump of saltbush, cold, hungry, and nearly dehydrated.

A knotted cord, images and emotions, slipped through my mind: The old lady—my grandfather's sister—crawling on hands and knees through the furnace heat of a summer day. Over scorching sand, through fields of tumbleweeds, over anthills, under barbed wire fences, across arroyos and the busy bus road. I pictured the thick calluses on her palms, and her face, darkened by the sun, seamed with wrinkles like the eroded foothills to the west. Her failing eyes, clouded and blinking behind thick glasses. Gray hair, once glossy black, in disarray, loosened in wisps from the woolen hair tie. And carrying on conversations with men and women long dead.

One time I had come across her crouching in a shallow ditch, cowering in terror. "*Yíiya, shiyázhí,*" she'd whispered. "*Naakai da shoołtse' lágo.*" There hadn't been any Mexican horsemen in the area for over three hundred years.

We walked slowly, swinging the beams of our flashlights back and forth. Voices called out now and then. "*Shimásání! Shimásání!*" Grandmother, grandmother. Some of the children whispered and giggled, but an adult voice hushed them. We might not see her, you carrying on like that! It was impossible to see anything besides the stars overhead and the flashlights bobbing in the darkness. In a few minutes, a pair of headlights swung out from the cluster of our houses and bounced toward us. There was no road so the vehicle maneuvered around sand hills and clumps of rabbitbrush. The long beams lit up the rugged slopes of the foothills a mile away.

"There she is!" someone shouted.

"*Shimásání!*"

"You dorks, it's just a piece of roofing paper!"

From the top of a low outcrop of clay, the headlights reached across the plain. The vehicle backed up slowly and swept its beams over the land. Then it descended and came toward us. In time, Grace, who was Frank's wife and my aunt, pulled up next to me in their truck. She rolled down her window and motioned to me. I went over, but she didn't say anything for a while. She stared out the windshield.

"You must think I'm awful," she said.

"No, Grace, I don't."

The truth was that I didn't, really. I understood more than she seemed to suppose. I waited. A burrowing owl called out, predicting more warm weather. A movement to the side caught my eye. "This flashlight of yours burned out," Frank said, handing me the cold object. I clicked it on and the filament in the bulb glowed a dull orange.

"I don't think we'll find her tonight," Frank said. "Best thing's to start again in the morning. Right now, she's holed up somewhere. We won't find her like that."

"You sure?" I asked, but I knew he was right. She would be too afraid to move. She would hide.

Grace sighed and pulled a tissue from the box on the dashboard. "It's sure as hell not easy," she said, her eyes glittering in the dim of the instrument panel. Frank shifted uneasily and looked away. He leaned against the cab. I excused myself to tell the others. As I walked away, I heard the truck door open.

"Sometimes I feel like quitting my job, but . . . " Grace said back at her house, waving her hand vaguely about the room as she poured coffee. I knew all about their situation and I could sympathize. Splinters and stone—that was rez life. Many families had gone to find better times in the cities, and those who stayed behind were left with the weight of holding things together. Frank and Grace had seven mouths to feed. And if that wasn't enough, the old lady had gone steadily downhill for a couple of years.

She'd cut quite a figure in her youth—a term I once heard her use—the first local woman to pluck her eyebrows and wear lipstick. Faux pearls. In one hand-tinted photograph she wore a fur stole, bobbed hair, and a Garbo-esque hat. Her acid wit had meant her dealings with men went strictly by her terms.

I once saw a tree fall. The feeling was like that. Within the past year, she had taken to the worrisome habit of leaving her house and crawling about outside, never mind the time or weather. It wasn't that she was deliberately neglected, however. The trouble was that she had to be watched constantly. The minute you turned your back, she was out the door. The responsibility could wear anyone down.

"I'm sick of the hour commute to Gallup, and then *this* happens," Grace said, sitting down across from me at the table. "I suppose I'll have to call in."

"No, don't do that," Frank told her. "I'll saddle up first thing in the morning. I'll find her."

Frank stood in the kitchen doorway, holding their youngest daughter, Faith, who was fast asleep. He carried her into the other room and Grace sighed, looking after them. She glanced at me, and I knew what she was thinking.

Frank had been unemployed for over three years now, ever since the uranium mines had closed. He'd gone around town with references from the employment office, but finally he had stopped knocking on doors. He never said anything about it, but I knew. It was easier to stay away from town than face the humiliation. And you didn't have to see the wealth and the way they treated people.

We walked a razor's edge. What else could we do? Every day we faced the thefts, the lies, and the hate. And there weren't too many things to do about it. Either you smiled and pretended it didn't matter, withdrew to where they couldn't reach you, or kissed ass. Or you went under. Half the boys I'd known in grade school were dead. The list was long: Despair. Self-hate. Alcohol. No work and plenty of time to stew. How would any man feel? He didn't have to tell me why he didn't meet the gaze of the rednecks in town, the tourists who asked to take the picture, or the contemptuous social workers who didn't understand.

"It's totally crazy," Grace said. Frank came back and sat next to her. "They're asleep," he said, indicating the children in the next room with a nod of his head.

"It's a dirty shame," said Frank. "In the old days, old folks stayed with family to the end."

"That's the old days," sighed Grace.

"Dead and buried," said Frank, shaking his head.

"Gone with the buffalo," I said.

Frank looked at me. He grinned. "Belly up," he said, holding out his hand and wiggling his fingers.

"A raw deal," I said.

"A bum steer."

"A crying shame."

"Honestly, you guys," Grace said.

"Just awful," said Frank, and eyed her sideways.

Grace made a funny sound and her shoulders began to jerk up and down. I thought she was crying, but she wasn't. "Utter tragedy," she gasped, and her throaty laugh swept us up. Soon we were whooping and snorting at the absurdity of us flopping helpless as hooked fish in the language.

After we calmed down, Grace brought more coffee and a plate of muffins. "Amazing, isn't it?" she said. "It started with Dick-and-Jane. Now, it's ship-the-old-lady-off-to-a-home."

"The Golden Years," Frank said.

"Shady Pines," I said.

"Okay, you two, that's enough," said Grace. "Let's get serious."

"If your sisters weren't such hang-around-the-fort Indians, you would have some help," Frank said.

"Now, Hon," Grace smiled. "They're making good money. You know they can't get that kind of lab work around here. And they'll help with the cost too, you know."

"I wish I could do something." Frank leaned back and ran his hand through his hair.

"You have the cattle to look after. I don't know what we would do if we didn't have the calves to sell in the fall. Besides, you look after the little ones when there's no sitter. How can I expect you to do all that and watch her, too?"

As I sat listening to them, I smelled the sharp odor of drying roots and wool. I heard the roof creak with the force of the wind. It was mid-winter and I was about five year old. Shimásání stood by the woodstove stirring something in a pot. The room was steamy and warm. She spoke in quiet voice, describing in our language how her grandmother had told of surviving the forced march to Fort Sumner, three hundred miles to the east. A hundred years after it had happened, the tragedy was fresh in her mind. "It was cold like that," she'd said, pointing with her lips toward the window to indicate the freezing wind outside. "The people walked the whole distance at gunpoint. Many bad things happened. If anyone paused to rest, they were shot. A woman who had stopped to give birth was impaled on a sword. Old people were abandoned and babies were clubbed. Vultures followed them all the way."

I drowsed on her lap, the crackle of the fire inside the iron stove lulling me within the womb-like embrace of her arms. The kerosene lamp cast a soft light on the log walls of her house.

There was a loom by her bed and she spent long hours each day weaving precious inches onto the rugs she made to sell. I played around her, making roads for my toy cars on the dirt floor. I stayed with her while my mother was at the hospital, a mysterious place I knew nothing about. After a while, she carried me to the bed and covered me with a quilt. Then she blew out the lamp and I went to sleep.

Now, her loom stood idle.

I saw what I had to do. "It's really for the best," I lied. "I mean, it's not doing her any good being out there. Think about winter, the storms, the hot stove. And you won't be the first ones to do it."

The words scraped my throat. Can you believe it, I thought. But these were modern times. The stars had shifted, my grandfather once said, and he didn't know what it meant.

The sink made a gurgling noise. We turned. The small panes of the window above the counter fractured our faces into a strange mosaic.

"Remember last month when she almost picked up that baby rattler?" Frank said. "At least she'll be safe in Chinle."

"Safe," Grace sighed. "Who would have thought that one day I would be the one? That she would turn into a child and that I would be the parent?"

"We have to do it, Grace. There's no choice." Frank touched her hand. A surge of anger rose inside me. They would never stop. The changes. The meddling. We were all affected, the men, the women, the children, and now, the elders.

I glanced up and saw Frank and Grace looking at me. I shrugged.

"Dammit," Grace said.

I studied the veins on the back of my hands.

The alarm rang at four. I rolled out of bed and quickly got dressed. I went out to greet the dawn with prayer and pollen. Then I put on the coffee and watched the all-night news on TV while I waited for sunrise. In New York City, blacks were protesting the killing of one of their young men by bat-wielding skinheads. The body of an undercover drug agent had been discovered in a shallow grave in Mexico. Outside, the rooster crowed and the clouds to the east slowly turned orange-pink.

The dog gruffed once and the gate hinges squeaked. Frank opened the door and came in. He rubbed his hands together and grinned.

"I found her," he said. "She was in the culvert under the bus road. Hell, I passed by there twice yesterday and didn't think to look inside it. She's home now, sipping coffee and munching warm tortillas like nothing happened." He laughed and shook his head. "That old lady is really something . . . " He looked out the window.

I couldn't help but smile.

I poured two cups of coffee and we watched the rest of the newscast. A suspended walkway in the atrium of the Kansas City Hyatt Regency had collapsed, killing several people and trapping scores of others under tons of steel and concrete. In Brazil, the Yanoama were protesting the destruction of their forest homeland. On the other side of the world, the Maori were threatening to disrupt a visit by the Queen.

SHIMÁSÁNÍ (Grandmother)

Gertrude Walters

Shimásání, you have traveled a long way—
From childhood
To Másání
Giving
Love
Protection
Understanding
And
Warmth.
Here I sit
Watching you
Sign documents
With your thumbprint
Trying hard to taste your life
Shimásání, you have traveled a long way—

▼ ▼ ▼ ▼ ▼ ▼

The Crystal Cave

Raven Hail

The whir of the window air conditioner was enough to lull anyone to sleep. David sat at his desk and tried to concentrate, but it was no use. He finally gave it up, shuffled a few papers on his desk, and walked out. He thought he had made it past the reception desk, but his secretary spied him. Practically nothing ever got past Miss Jamieson.

She would never ask, but her raised eyebrows indicated her curiosity.

"I thought I might leave a little early and take my son down to the river-bank. He's anxious to try out his new fishing pole."

"Well, watch yourself so you don't get sidetracked by that new widder Mankiller's house on the way."

"The name is Sixkiller," he patiently pointed out.

"Oh, excuse me. It's just that everyone seems to have business over that way ever since she moved in. You'd think no one had ever seen a Cherokee Indian before."

"Well," he grinned, "I think I should do the neighborly thing and drop in and borrow a cup of bourbon."

"It's a cup of sugar," she corrected him.

"You borrow what you like, I'll borrow what I like. I can do more with a cup of bourbon," was his parting shot as he went out to his car.

It was a perfect day for driving along the countryside. He hadn't really meant to stop, but he wasn't in any particular hurry, and he saw Robin Sixkiller in the front yard pulling weeds.

"How's the weed business?" he greeted her. "I hear you've got a weed for every need!"

"What do you need?"

"I'll take a pound of marijuana." he said. "That's the 'in' thing at the moment, isn't it?"

"I'm fresh out."

"Then what do you have that's good on the market?"

"Oh, there's some sage, and that's rosemary," she pointed out.

"What's the rosemary good for?"

"It's good for making tea," she explained. "Would you like to try some rosemary tea?"

“Sounds good—if it’s not too much trouble.” He followed her into the house and settled down in an easy chair, making himself comfortably at home. Before he had time to finish his first cigarette, she reappeared with two frosty glasses of a somewhat cloudy liquid, complete with ice cubes.

“Looks like lemonade.” He sampled it. “Tastes like lemonade, too. It’s delicious.”

“I added some lemon and honey. Most people like it that way.”

“Then would you call it rosemary tea with lemon, or lemonade flavored with rosemary?”

She laughed. “I hadn’t thought of it that way.”

“Will it make me healthy, wealthy, or wise?”

“Rosemary is for remembrance. It’s not supposed to give you any more knowledge, but to allow you to remember what you already know. Of course, too much of it might remember you right out of this world.”

“Already I remember something,” he said, “that I hadn’t thought of in years. It was somewhere right in this area, too. They used to say that there was an old cave hidden somewhere—a long time ago. Full of gold and silver and all kinds of treasure. When I was a kid I used to spend whole afternoons looking for it. Found lots of wonderful treasures, too, like big fat bullfrogs, and shells, and arrowheads, and juicy blackberries. I combed the countryside, far and wide. But of course there was no cave. It was just a wonderful fantasy to think and dream about.”

There was a comfortable silence as if both withdrew into individual thought. Then, as if reaching a decision, she said, “There is a cave. I know where it is.”

He wondered if she could possibly be serious. “Where is it?”

“Next to the springs.”

He shook his head. “I looked there.” Then, as an afterthought, “How did you find it?”

“There is an old Indian legend that people originally came to Earth from the Pleiades Star Cluster. They traveled through space by the use of solar energy. When their mission was completed, they went back to the Pleiades. While those first people were here, they lived underground. That’s why I am here—because the cave is here.”

“Of course, you know I don’t believe you. Will you show it to me?”

“Yes.”

“Right now? Today?”

“No, not today. But one day I will show it to you.”

“Oh, someday,” he countered. “That’s what they always say. Always some-day—but never today.”

"You don't believe me."

"I'll believe it when I see it." He settled back into the chair, as if that ended the matter.

To his surprise, she slipped on her moccasins, stood up, and started for the door. "Come on."

He had a comfortable feeling of lethargy, as if he were about to doze off sitting in the chair. When he stood up he felt a tingling sensation at the tips of his fingers and toes as if they had gone to sleep while he was sitting there. He roused himself and followed her through the open door and down along the path. The sun was a great round ball of flame as it hovered over the horizon.

"It's a little late in the day to go poking around caves," he observed. "Or is it dark in the daytime, too? I didn't think to bring my flashlight."

"We'll be able to see," she assured him. "We won't go all the way through—not today. It wouldn't be a good idea. Some other time we'll start earlier and take the grand tour. But now we can just satisfy your curiosity that it's there."

They reached the springs and she walked a few feet past. She lifted aside the lush growth of wild grapes and waited for him to come alongside. He could see nothing, and wondered if she had been only teasing after all.

"Take my hand," she cautioned, "and don't let go of it until we get back out here."

"Why?"

"We might get separated and you don't want to go wandering around a strange cave all by yourself."

"Think I might panic?" He smiled at the idea.

"No, I just wanted to hold your hand, and that's the best excuse I could think of."

"You don't need an excuse."

"Well, then—ask a silly question and you get a silly answer."

She took his hand and went behind the vines, pulling him after her. He couldn't see a thing and the leaves and tendrils brushed along his face and arms. Then she came to a full stop, and in the smothering darkness he felt something crawling along the back of his neck. Thinking it must be a spider or some creepy-crawly thing, he slapped at it and it squashed in his hand. He brought his hand around in front of him and felt the frustration of not being able to see it. The sudden light gave him the impression that it was blood and goo. But it was only purple grape juice. He had caught a grape and squashed it. Only then did he realize that they were in the cave and there was light. He looked for the source but could not find it. It was not bright; he realized it had only appeared so at first because of the contrast from complete darkness. It was a hazy, diffused light everywhere, except for a shining crystal stone near the entrance.

The walls were perfectly straight—too straight to be natural formation. And all the way around were figures of animals and birds and people, possibly—or partially. He started around the walls to examine them more closely, and she followed along. In the muted light he couldn't tell whether it was painting or carving. The cavern was not very large, but it seemed larger because there was nothing in it but a large stone table with a bowl on it and a stool behind it. The bowl was large and ornate. It looked like copper. It was carved like a coiled snake, with the head extending outward from the rim at the top. With two shining eyes staring straight into his eyes.

It looked so real that he reached out to feel of it to make sure. He had the distinct feeling that the head was moving forward to meet his hand, when suddenly the light went out. It so startled him that he jumped away, tripped over the stool, and fell flat on the floor. In the complete silence and darkness he lay perfectly still and tried to think what to do next. Then there was a faint sound, like a dried leaf scraping over stone. He crawled frantically in the opposite direction to get away, until his head bumped against the wall. He was stunned, and hesitated until the pain subsided, and then realized that he had lost his bearings and had no idea which way was out. He lay there, petrified with pain and fright, while the scraping sound came closer and closer. Then her hand touched his shoulder and followed it down to take his hand. She helped him to his feet and guided him gently to the entrance, through the vines, and out into the open air.

The sun had set and through the gathering twilight they walked silently back to the house. Not a word had been spoken since they first entered the cave. The evening noises of the birds and little forest animals settling in for the night were a welcome normal sound. A bullfrog called out, "rivet," and another answered back.

By the time they reached the back door, he was feeling a little foolish.

"Well," he said, "you do put on a good show."

"Would you like another cup of tea?"

"Tea? No, thanks. I think I'll stick to Scotch and soda from now on. It may give me delusions and hallucinations, but they're the kind I'm used to."

"Scotch and soda it is, then. I think I'll have some coffee, through, because I have much to do tonight and I'll be up until all hours."

"Where did the light come from?" he asked. "Did you just say 'Let there be light' and there it was?"

"No," she smiled. "It isn't quite that simple—but really no great mystery after all. Did you notice the crystal stone at the entrance? There is an opening to the outside on the opposite wall. You don't notice it outside because it's near the springs. When the sun is at a certain spot near the horizon, and the stone is placed in the right position, it catches the light directly from the sun and the facets of the stone reflect the light throughout the cavern. So—I push the stone, and the lights go on!"

"Not magic, huh?" he mused. "Then why did the lights go out? There's no way you could have pushed that stone again."

"That's right," she agreed. "But don't be a button-down mind. Just because I turned on the light doesn't mean that I also turned it off."

"It turned itself off?"

"Well, you might say that—in a way. You see, the sun disappeared below the horizon. And the moment there was no more sun—no more light."

He thought about it while he sipped his drink. "You know, I must have panicked. I heard a noise and thought it was that snake coming after me."

"Like this?" She slid her moccasin across the bare floor. "That was me looking for you. It's a good thing you bumped your head and stayed put, or we might be there yet, playing follow-the-leader around and around and around."

"It all sounds so natural and reasonable, the way you explain it." He put down his empty glass and went to the front door.

"Do you always leave your doors open—even when you're out?"

"Only on Midsummer's Eve," she admitted.

"Is that one of your holidays? Were you expecting someone?"

"Not really. It's just an old superstition, so old nobody knows how it started. Midsummer's Eve, they say, is when the Little People walk along their paths to get to—wherever it is that Little People go; and if a house is on their path and the doors are open, they walk right through and go on about their business. But if the doors are closed, they tear the house down or burn it up, or push it out of the way."

"And this house is on the fairy path?"

"I can't say that it is," she said. "But on the other hand, I can't say for sure that it isn't."

"Do you really believe that stuff?"

"I like to. I understand that these old superstitions work just the same, whether you believe them or not." She shrugged. "Anyway, the breeze is wonderful on a hot night. And what could I possibly have here that anyone would bother to steal?"

"You. You could be murdered in your bed, you know."

"Do people murder people around here?"

"Only witches on Midsummer's Eve," he said. Then he waved goodbye and walked away into the summer night.

He had reached his own front door and was fumbling for the key when a thought struck him. He had completely forgotten to borrow the cup of bourbon. Oh well, he'd just have to go back for another visit. Things were certainly looking up for the rest of the long hot summer.

▼ ▼ ▼ ▼ ▼ ▼

Southwest Navajo Moonlight

Vee F. Browne

Open the door to the sights and sounds of the Southwest, where Mr. Coyote the trickster tells the story.

"This is the most beautiful Coyote's den on the whole Mother Earth. The Butte Gods reign over our desert site. The clouds are only for picture taking—never giving enough rain, except when the Pueblos request it," Coyote boasted.

"There's coyote in all of us; there is a lesson to be learned"—his most profound notorious phrase.

Suddenly, a devil's twister slams the Southwest door, and Coyote prances over to open the turquoise door. He returns to his hump, making himself comfortable, while crossing his thin pelt legs. From his adobe surroundings, he gazes at the full Navajo moon.

"You may look at the Anasazi Ruins, Canyon De Chelly, and our pottery shards, but *dare not* take our artifacts. The Kachina Gods will ask you to bring them back," Coyote warned, gently pawing his bristly whiskers. "Ah-h-oow. There are golden moments here in the Southwest. We enjoy making love in the washbeds, under the juniper trees, with fine sand rubbing our bare bottoms, while romantically being touched by the Navajo moonlight."

Shuffling his thin legs, he smirks and lifts his snout into the air, saying, "I wouldn't be anywhere but the Southwest. Ah-h-oow, Ah-h-oow! There is no place like it. It's the best!"

This thought tickles his heart, mind and soul. At last, he dozes off and dreams of the sights and sounds of the tourists.

"Don't you just love the tourist season?" he mumbles in his sleep, as his restless legs jerk. "We sell tribal jewelry, books, sand paintings, indigenous food, and pottery. But, most of all we sell ourselves, our talents, and charisma. And now that you know of the sights and sounds and *sales* in the Southwest, make your reservations now and *be here!*"

In his dream Coyote reaches for his no-name brand cigarette and a glass of José Cuervo on the rocks. One shot is all it takes. He grins from jowl to jowl.

"Southwest is *big time! This* is *the* meeting place!" Coyote calls out chuckles with a hiss. Now he feels mellow. "We play dangerously. We're sly. We gamble, and even play *jackpot!*" He smirks and opens one lazy drowsy amber eye.

The sights and sounds and sales of the Southwest will soon close its doors for the winter season.

"Hibernation time!" Coyote says, wagging his trickster tail, "until next season."

Will you dare open the door to the sights and sounds of the Southwest, and take a Navajo moonbath come spring?

▼ ▼ ▼ ▼ ▼ ▼

AUGUST

Irvin Morris

The myriad boughs and branches in the forest bent with the weight of water droplets that formed continuously from the moisture in the air and the misting low clouds that hid the sun for four days in a row until the land was soaked and could absorb no more and shed the rain as it fell so that streams sloughed off hillsides and meadows in wide rippling sheets across clearings that were funnels for the water that besieged yet cleaned the land including the three stark white tipis that rose among the dark pines at the edge of the clearing where songs and prayers would ring out at dusk though for now it was so quiet and only the hiss of gentle rain was heard until late afternoon when waterdrums and gourd rattles rose above the murmur of voices and laughter as some of the men practiced for the night-long service that would end at daybreak with a feast that the women were busy preparing even as the children pestered and complained and galloped around as if they smelled the special freedom like horses scent water but the women wore patience in smiles and indulgence as small brown hands grabbed tidbits off tabletops as the cooks reveled in the congeniality of gossip and excited gestures of flour-speckled hands that marked explosive mirth as someone told a good one about the lost tourist and the reservation gingerbread man or the even better one about the old days and rain and salamanders which left them in stitches waving their hands helplessly until cramps quelled them long enough to overhear the conversations outside of young people talking about rock music and the best bands and the baddest hairstyles and so forth as the afternoon grew dim closer to dusk when fires were lit inside the tipis which then glowed like Chinese lanterns or shadow theaters that kept children busy guessing who was which shape on the stretched canvas until they grew sleepy and drifted off to their beds and the Fire Chief stoked a fire that would burn all night with unbridled power rising up to console and inflame with allusions to warmth and the sun shining as fierce as hope and stars had it been clear they might have glimpsed through the smoke-hole where the poles were tied together into a brace strong enough to withstand high winds though that wouldn't happen everyone said as they dressed in fine clothes and jewelry and hats and hairdos that were in style like woven vests and ropers and nugget turquoises that would gleam in the flickering firelight as the service commenced with drumbeats and tobacco and feelings of goodwill like cedar incense upon the assembled and they leaned forward in earnest prayer or just gazed into the dancing flames and the glowing bed of embers banked against the low altar of sand laid down and tamped into a long narrow crescent that held a single line drawn across the top end to end representing life above the burgeoning lake of ashes that filled the hollow of the crescent with grays and muted blacks and whites that mimicked the pattern on someone's Pendleton or hat or jacket from Hudson's Bay which also echoed the gray of embers and muted night infused with good thoughts and songs and prayer until suddenly without warning a woman screamed and stood up shaking her shawl exclaiming how cold the thing had been which grazed her and the excitement spread and soon they stuffed their fine Pendletons into the openings along the bottom of the tipis to keep out the intruders whose translucent buff or gray bodies alarmed them maybe on account of the joke about rain and women and salamanders or just on account of their appearance looking the way they did crouching low and moving about in the dancing firelight like alligators hissing and arching their backs.

▼ ▼ ▼ ▼ ▼ ▼

Lakota Warrior

For my father *(Oglala Lakota)*

Arthur J. Harvey

My Lakota father
War hero
Drafted at 21
Thrust into oblivion
Regimented trained
Small skinny
In crisp army green
Always smiling fresh
Tentatively
Remembrance
Of drunken rage
Crying
For people
Slain
Korean children
Spookily familiar
Like ones
Left at home

Heat of war
Extreme cold

Slivers in legs
Unconscious memories
"hit the deck"
My brothers are dead
Useless medals
Army suits
Burned
Silver medal
Bronze medal
Lost
Lost blackness
Six months
He did not complain
Only saluted
At moment of death.

▼ ▼ ▼ ▼ ▼ ▼

Neon Powwow

Dan L. Crank

In the dark interior of the side street bar, and along the wall in the narrow drinking place, there were dark forms sitting sluggishly or hunched over whatever they were nursing. Empty beer bottles and cans and food crumbs littered the tables. Afternoon light flooded in the open doorway and glints of passing automobiles reflected into the dark room. An Indian guy who chain-smoked nonfiltered Camels sat in a booth near the bright entrance. His cigarette smoke played in the sunbeams. Joe Bluesky sat with a college crowd in the last booth. The barkeep stood behind an old wooden bar made vintage by beer stains, elbows, and greasy food. It was polished to a high gloss with constant rubbings of arms and elbows of numerous past patrons. The bar had supported countless drunk Indians and Mexicans, and occasionally a drunk white man with Indian friends. A red and blue neon Coors sign flickered a little and buzzed and fizzled when it did not flash.

At Bluesky's table were two Navajo college girls, Joe's buddy who only drank canned Coors, and a Hopi guy who attended the same college. The Hopi was bent over, a bottle of longnecked Bud pressed his cheek. He had held that posture for some time now. He stirred and raised his arm for the last gulp from his bottle.

"Damn," he said. "I think I'm getting wasted," he said to Darlene, one of the Navajo girls. She ignored his bloodshot stare and his crazy grin.

"I think he is dead drunk," Joe commented.

"He was already that way when I met him back on campus," said the other Navajo guy.

The Hopi stirred again, looked up, and laughed. He said, "Now I am *more* drunk. I drank more than you guys, you don't drink fast enough. What kind of Navajos are you?"

"Don't worry," said Joe's buddy. "I only drink fast when I am on a reservation. I'd rather be caught with the liquor in my stomach than in my hands."

"Bull," said the Hopi.

Joe and his buddy laughed out loud.

The chain smoker at the front booth looked around and then lit another cigarette. The early afternoon crowd was thin.

Darlene and Laura looked at the Hopi, then at each other. Laura especially didn't want to waste another Saturday evening, like last weekend. They had drunk stale beer in their apartment while studying for some exams. By the time they got to an Indian bar, their friends had left and gone elsewhere. The girls had sat and endured bleary-eyed drunks and other individuals who had gone over the edge and barely hung on.

Today it might be different. This old place was actually nicer than the other bars lining the front and main side streets. The crowd could drink well and if they got hungry and couldn't walk, they could order microwaved pizza. The barkeep also kept some old-fashioned dilled eggs in large jars on the bar. Serious drinking was accomplished here. In dorms and apartments, everybody drank to get drunk quickly and what subsequently followed was rowdiness. Laura liked this bar. At all the bars, men were always trying to engage in a conversation with the girls or get dates with them. Usually a game ensued where they pretended they were waiting for someone, or that they were their male friends' wives. Joe's Navajo buddy was one of Laura's regular make-believe husbands.

Like the Hopi guy, he was nice and intelligent when he wasn't in his present condition. Laura liked Joe Bluesky, too. She knew Joe from a previous party when he was a student. One day Joe quit attending classes and went back to the reservation. Or someone had said that Joe had gone back to herd sheep. He had kept in touch, though. Now here he was—back for a visit, and he was buying. . . . He also looked good and fit in long hair and faded Levi clothing. The Hopi guy was ragged and wasted compared to Joe. Now Darlene and Laura were the Hopi's only audience as he slowly drank himself into oblivion. When he finally slumped over, perhaps they might celebrate.

Joe said, "I have known some great Indian drinkers with great outlooks on life but they are usually the worst drinkers."

"The quiet ones are the best," Darlene said as she looked at Joe.

Laura then squealed with laughter. She said, "You mean sexually, or as conversationalists?"

"No, you idiot," Darlene replied. "I mean that the quiet Indian guys are the ones that get deep and meaningful."

"You're still talking about sex, aren't you?" Laura again asked. She laughed even louder.

Joe's buddy took a deep drink. He grinned at Laura and Darlene. He then said, "Darlene is talking about both. Either way it's a f---ing shame some of us don't get pissing philosophical when we're f---ing sober."

"You're getting real vulgar," Laura said.

He retorted, "Vulgarity breaks the ice and drives home the point, and it breaks the stereotype of the non-swearing quiet Indian."

"He's getting philosophical now, and you're touching a nerve, Laura," said Joe.

The Hopi then raised his head and said, "I want to get deep and meaningful, and I want to be touched." He laughed in a silly high voice, and pushed his point further. "First I want to get philosophical, and then I want to see if I can get laid."

The group looked at each other. The Hopi seemed to be getting a second life. It was an event to drink to. Joe's buddy ordered another round. Their table was littered with bottles and cans.

The barkeep was an old Mexican guy with thinning hair and he had the skin coloring of someone who had lived in a cave or a dark interior for years. He spoke several basic Indian greetings and looked like someone's Navajo grandfather. He spoke good Navajo and exchanged jokes with some of the regulars. He placed the tray of drinks on the table and passed a beer to everyone at Joe's table. He then cleaned up a little and took the empties with him. On his way back he checked each patron's beer level or mental state for later reference. The early Saturday afternoon was not busy. Some patrons stopped only for one drink, then they were off to other beer joints. It was still cruising time; the Indians were looking for a good Coors crowd, and the white college students wanted cheap Mexican food to eat with their trendy Tecates.

The drinks to celebrate the Hopi's revival were drained. Silence again set in. The Hopi excused himself and left the table with a slight stagger. He ran his hand along the wooden bar and walked up to the doorway. He stood there and shaded his eyes against the bright afternoon light. Then he walked back toward their table and passed it. The restroom's door slammed loudly.

"He's okay now," said Joe's buddy. "He was ready to go out. It saves us the trouble of baby-sitting him."

Darlene took a cigarette out of a crumpled pack on the table. She lit it and inhaled deeply. Laura watched the smoke curl and remain in the air. The smoke took the stale odor of the bar away momentarily.

Laura then took Darlene's cigarette and took a drag on it.

"Well, I guess we can cruise on, then," Joe Bluesky said.

"Where to?" asked Laura.

"Anyone hungry?" Joe asked. "We could check out that old Chinese cafe on Aspen Street; the one where there are old photographs of Navajo railroad workers."

"That was some history and they were some drinkers," his buddy said. "I read someplace where these guys worked six days a week, then came into town on Saturday nights to have a wild time. Then they stayed wasted until it was time to go back to work Monday mornings."

The chain smoker in the front of the bar got up and moved about, then he took one of his cigarettes and went out the door.

"Now you have become a historian," Laura said to the Navajo guy.

"I was only giving you some unsubstantiated fiction," he replied.

"It sounds good, like real history," added Darlene.

"Watch out for him; he is the quiet type." Laura commented. She looked at the Navajo guy. "He might become a deep historian and a meaningful philosopher."

He said, "Someday, maybe someday."

The Hopi took a long time to relieve or revive himself. Joe and his buddy became concerned. Joe Bluesky stood up, and stepped over Laura's right leg and foot, the one that Laura had been brushing against him most of the afternoon. He made his way to the bathroom.

Bluesky opened the rough door and stepped into the silent room. One of the faucets dripped slowly, the moist air was slowly sucked outside through the stained vents. A fly buzzed in front of the mirror, darting at its own image. Joe dropped to one knee and looked under the stalls. He saw the Hopi's legs in the last one. His pants were down around the ankles, and the contents of his pockets were spilled out on the floor. It was too quiet. Joe started sweating. All of a sudden, the beer-contaminated blood rushed to his head and awakened him. The faucet dripped louder into the worn and chipped basin, and it reverberated in Joe's head.

▼ ▼ ▼ ▼ ▼ ▼

The Coffee Maker

Melissa A. Pope

the sound of the coffee maker won't leave my thoughts behind and the longer I listen the more   wine   I have to make more and more cliché lines into poetry to relive my lonely summer room heater & coffee maker and shades closed to take   away the light in my mirror any name is spoken but I forgot my own name and the creatures run across my room and plant my mind with dreams the world will end the coffee maker sits on the floor the sound of it not making a gurgle spilling out the sound in a dark room with a space heater in the hot afternoon of a summer the sound of a coffee maker the sound of a coffee maker as I watch it sitting on my floor its getting ready to pour into my green beer mugs as I sip my wine as I swallow   my   sleeping pills.

▼ ▼ ▼ ▼ ▼ ▼

How to Be a Southwest Indigenous Writer

Vee F. Browne

Live in the Southwest, near a mesa, butte, or plateau. Follow the art of the indigenous writer. Talk to the mesa every morning before dawn. Sit on a rock facing the East. Pick up the dirt and let it run through your fingers; throw some to the East, West, South, and North Gods. Be still and stay loose. Learn to watch lambs *(dibe y'zhi)*. Plant a tumbleweed garden. Invite a black hair charmer to Navajo tea. Write *yes* with cedar beads. Type *yes!* one full page each day before dawn. Make friends with the deities and coyote. Dream as you drive down the dirt road. Look forward to the female rain, where colorful beads make up the rainbow. Cry during movies—*Thunderheart, Powwow Highway, Dances with Wolves, The Last of the Mohicans, Soldier Blue, Man Called Horse, Little Big Horn,* and *Chief Crazy Horse.* Scream and cheer at the Indian National Finals Rodeo in November. Roll in the snow. Hike as high as you can on the San Francisco Peaks by moonlight. Meet publishers with a smile. Believe you're a damn good writer. Scribble on napkins. Carry broken lead pencils. Wear a turquoise watch. Don't wash your face before you type. Eat buttered popcorn for lunch with Diet Coke. Make friends with liberty and ambiguity. Wear a writer's attitude. Refuse to follow the norm. Refuse to see black and white; see gray. Know there are no definite answers. Do not question your intuition. Nap under a juniper tree. Do it now—begin it and royalties will follow. Laugh often. Sit under the Navajo moon each month. Think possibilities always. Wear moccasins. Write whatever you dream. Let editors correct you. Don't be hurt. Say to yourself, I'll try again. Rewrite and rewrite. Believe in ceremonies. Talk to the stars. Wave to the pink skies and sunset. Sit and talk with the elders. Giggle with kindergartners. Hold babies to the sky in gratitude. Start your mornings with an address to Sunbearer. Wear ghost beads and a turquoise nugget. Let nothing disturb your peace of mind. Stay warm, content, and optimistic. Draw on the canyon walls. Read every other day. Imagine yourself as creator of fiction and nonfiction stories. Jump without fear. Listen to the Wind Gods. Play with words. Tell coyote jokes. Fantasize. Write for your inner child. Build a hooghan with Navajo Pendleton blankets. Hug sand lizards. Share your fried bread with a kangaroo rat. Write romantic letters with poetry of the indigenous people. Take long walks alone. Talk on the phone for seven hours to a dear friend. Ride rams and goats. Talk about the novel. Refuse to be late for Writer's Workshop. Look for characters in your friends. Let it go! Get permission from the Spider People to tell your stories during the winter season. Listen for the first thunder in February. Write to enjoy and weave a rug with words. Listen to what the Coyote has to say. Be honest to one person. *Taa'a kodi ahe'hee!* The End

▼ ▼ ▼ ▼ ▼ ▼

The Contributors

HEATHER PAKANALI AHTONE is Choctaw and Chickasaw. She was born in Minnesota in 1968 but has lived throughout the Midwest and Southwest. She writes plays as well as poetry. She also does performance pieces for stage and video. She hopes to work professionally with theater and video.

RACHAEL ARVISO, Navajo and Zuni, lives and works on the Navajo Reservation with her family. "The Crows" is her first short story.

ESTHER G. BELIN is Navajo and has a B.A. from the University of California at Berkeley. She is currently living in Oakland.

VEE F. BROWNE has been writing for about three years. She is Navajo, from the Cottonwood-Salina area, and her clans are Bitter Water and Water Flows Together. She is the author of a children's book, *Monster Slayer* (published by Northland Publishing), which has won national recognition; the sequel, *Monster Birds*, will be published in the fall of 1993.

DAN L. CRANK lives in Dennehotso, Arizona. He is of the Bitahni clan and born for the Kinlichiiini clan. He has an M.A. in educational foundations. He has been previously published .

ROSEMARY DIAZ is Tewa from Santa Clara Pueblo in New Mexico. She lives and works in Santa Fe. She received her bachelor's degree in creative writing from the University of California at Santa Cruz in 1992. Her work has been included in numerous Indian periodicals.

DELLA FRANK is Navajo and is presently living in Aneth, Utah, where she was born. She has three children. She has a B.S., two M.A. degrees, and a terminal degree. She is working on a third M.A. She says, "I hope to echo the voices of women across the Native American continent in my writing."

GEORGEANN GREGORY teaches at the University of New Mexico.

RAVEN HAIL has lived in the Southwest for some time. She is originally from Oklahoma and has been published previously. She is a lecturer and writer on American Indian culture. She is Cherokee and not only writes, but sings and gives presentations on dancing, folklore, and history.

ARTHUR J. HARVEY was born and raised on the Pine Ridge Reservation. He is Oglala Sioux and is twenty-eight years old. What brought him to the Southwest was the landscape and a desire to become a voice of Native American people through his writing. This is his first published work.

A. A. HEDGE COKE is Huron/Tsalagi/French Canadian/Portuguese. She has been previously published in several small press magazines. She lives in Santa Fe.

LORENZO BACA is Isleta Pueblo and Mescalero Apache. He was born in Arizona and educated in New Mexico and California. He has a master of arts degree from UCLA in American Indian studies. He not only writes but is also a performing and visual artist who does fine art, sculpture, video, storytelling, and acting.

NANCY MARYBOY is of Navajo and Cherokee descent. She lives on the Navajo Reservation and is involved in photography, writing, teaching, and a wide range of other interests. She has an M.F.A. in creative writing. She writes poetry as well as short stories.

IRVIN MORRIS is a Navajo from Tohatchi, New Mexico. His clans are Tabaahi and Totshonii. He has an A.F.A., B.F.A., and M.F.A. At present he is working at Cornell University. Soon he will begin work on a doctorate in Native American studies. He says, "What I am and what I write about arises out of that (reservation) experience. I write about what I see and what I know. I write to honor the things I am most proud of: my language, my culture, and my people. Whatever else I may do, I will always write." He is one of a growing number of Navajos writing in their own language.

MELISSA A. POPE is an Objibwe Indian from the Great Lakes area. She is a dancer as well as a writer and is in the creative writing program of the Institute of American Indian Arts.

PATROCLUS EUGENE SAVINO is a pen name for a Navajo writer who grew up in northwestern New Mexico in a place called the Checker Board Area. He has been writing short stories and throwing them away since high school. He has been published in Japan and France.

KAREN AND WALLY STRONG live and work in Santa Fe, New Mexico. Karen is Haida and Wally is Yakima from Washington state. Both are involved in teaching and keeping traditional values alive through playwriting.

BRENT TOADLENA is a Navajo from Chinle, Arizona. At present he is going to school in Santa Fe, New Mexico.

STACEY VELARDE is from Albuquerque, New Mexico. She was born in 1968 and is a member of the Jicarilla Apache Tribe, which is located in Dulce, New Mexico. She has been around horses for most of her life and has competed in professional rodeo since she was thirteen. This background was the inspiration for the story "Carnival Lights." She hopes to graduate from the University of New Mexico late this year.

CARLSON VICENTI is an Apache from Dulce, New Mexico. Right now he is temporarily located in Vancouver, British Columbia. He says that he tries to write about Native Americans in modern times as the people incorporate traditional ways in modern life.

GERTRUDE WALTERS is Navajo and lives in Canoncito, New Mexico with her husband and two children, Sage and Eric. She has been writing poetry since she was a teenager and says that it has kept her strong in stressful times. This is her first published work.

FLOYD D. YAZZIE resides in Many Farms, Arizona. He is working toward a B.A. in English. His interest in writing is new. He has attended the Fashion Institute of Design in Los Angeles and the University of Arizona.

▼ ▼ ▼ ▼ ▼ ▼

THE EDITOR

ANNA LEE WALTERS, who is Pawnee/Otoe, is an English instructor at Navajo Community College in Tsaile, Arizona. In addition to being published in numerous journals and anthologies, she has authored or edited several books, including *The Sacred: Ways of Knowledge, Sources of Life; The Sun Is Not Merciful* (a short story collection); *The Spirit of Native America: Beauty and Mysticism in American Indian Art;* the novel *Ghost Singer; Talking Indian: Reflections on Writing and Survival;* and the children's book *The Two-Legged Creature: An Otoe Story.*